CONGRESSIONAL POLICIES, PRACTICES AND PROCEDURES

THE HOUSE OF REPRESENTATIVES: APPORTIONMENT AND REDISTRICTING

Congressional Policies, Practices and Procedures

Additional books in this series can be found on Nova's website under the Series tab.

Additional E-books in this series can be found on Nova's website under the E-books tab.

CONGRESSIONAL POLICIES, PRACTICES AND PROCEDURES

THE HOUSE OF REPRESENTATIVES: APPORTIONMENT AND REDISTRICTING

ROLAND D. ORSINO
AND
OLIVIA G. TRANCE
EDITORS

Nova Science Publishers, Inc.
New York

For permission to use material from this book please contact us:
Telephone 631-231-7269; Fax 631-231-8175
Web Site: http://www.novapublishers.com

NOTICE TO THE READER

Library of Congress Cataloging-in-Publication Data

The House of Representatives : apportionment and controversies / editors, Roland D. Orsino and Olivia G. Trance.
p. cm.
Includes bibliographical references and index.
ISBN 978-1-61324-308-4 (hardcover : alk. paper) 1. United States. Congress. House--Election districts. 2. Apportionment (Election law)--United States. 3. Election districts--United States. 4. United States--Census, 2010. I. Orsino, Roland D. II. Trance, Olivia G.
JK1341.H68 2011
328.73'07345--dc22

2011012578

Published by Nova Science Publishers, Inc. † New York

CONTENTS

PREFACE

The Constitution requires that states be represented in the House of Representatives in accordance with their population. It also requires that each state have at least one Representative, and that there be no more than one Representative for every 30,000 persons. For the 2010 apportionment, this could have meant a House of Representatives as small as 50 or as large as 10,306 Representatives. This book examines apportioning seats in the House of Representatives among the states in proportion to state population as required by the Constitution, which appears to be a simple task. In fact, however, the Constitution presented Congress with issues that have provoked extended and recurring debate, which are discussed in this compilation.

Chapter 1- On December 21, 2010, the number of seats allocated to each state for the House of Representatives was announced. This allocation likely will determine representation to the House for the next five Congresses.

The Constitution requires that states be represented in the House of Representatives in accord with their population. It also requires that each state have at least one Representative, and that there be no more than one Representative for every 30,000 persons. For the 2010 apportionment, this could have meant a House of Representatives as small as 50 or as large as 10,306 Representatives.

Chapter 2- On December 21, 2010, the Commerce Department released 2010 Census population figures and the resulting reapportionment of seats in the House of Representatives. The apportionment population of the 50 states in 2010 is 309,183,463, a figure 9.9% greater than in 2000. Just as in the 108th Congress, 12 seats will shift among 18 states in the 113th Congress as a result of the reapportionment. The next census data release will begin February

2011, when the Census Bureau will provide states the small-area data necessary to re-draw congressional and state legislative districts in time for the 2012 elections.

Chapter 3- Apportionment Population and Number of Representatives by State 2010 census.

Chapter 4- Apportionment of the U.S. House of Representatives based on 2010 census

Chapter 5- Overseas Population of the 50 States and the District of Columbia 2010 census

Chapter 6- Change in Number of States in the U.S. House of Representatives, by State, seats gained and lost ,1940 to 2010

Chapter 7- Change in Number of States in the U.S. House of Representatives, by Region,1940 to 2010

Chapter 8- In preparation for the reallocation of Representatives among the states based on the 2010 Census, it may prove helpful to examine the current House of Representatives apportionment formula. In addition, some members of the statistical community have, in the recent past, urged Congress to consider changing the current apportionment formula. Consequently, an examination of other methods that could be used to apportion the seats in the House of Representatives may contribute to a deeper understanding of the apportionment process.

Chapter 9- In the 2010 decennial census, the Census Bureau will attempt to count the total population of the United States. This includes, as in previous censuses, all U.S. citizens, lawfully present aliens, and unauthorized aliens. Some have suggested excluding aliens, particularly those who are in the country unlawfully, from the census count, in part so that they would not be included in the data used to apportion House seats among the states and determine voting districts within them.

Chapter 10- Two proposals (H.R. 157 / S. 160) have been introduced in the 111th Congress to provide for voting representation in the U.S. House of Representatives for the residents of the District of Columbia (DC). H.R. 157 /S. 160, for purposes of voting representation, treat the District of Columbia as if it were a state, giving a House seat to the District, but restricting it to a single seat under any future apportionments. The bills also would increase the size of the House to 437 members from 435, and give the additional seat to the state of Utah. This report shows the distribution of House seats based on the 2000 census for 435 seats and for 437 seats as specified in the proposal. The report also examines the impact of using the 2009 estimated population to allocate the 437 seats, including the single seat provided to the District in the 2010 reapportionment.

Chapter 11- For years, the people of the Commonwealth of Puerto Rico have been involved in discussions relating to changing the political status of Puerto Rico from a commonwealth of the United States to either the 51st state or an independent nation, or maintaining the status quo as a commonwealth.

In the 111th Congress, H.R. 2499, introduced by Representative Pedro Pierluisi, would establish procedures to determine Puerto Rico's political status. It would authorize a two-stage plebiscite in Puerto Rico to reconsider the status issue. H.R. 2499 is similar to H.R. 900 as introduced in the 110th Congress. A possible outcome of this process is Puerto Rican statehood.

Chapter 12- Once every 10 years, Americans stand up to be counted. Downtown and out-of-town, in the mountains and on the farms, we speak up and let our governments know that we intend to be represented in the decisions that they make.

The census gives us an opportunity to be part of the democratic process. Census numbers ensure that our representative districts—for the U.S. Congress and for state legislatures, and in our city and town governments—reflect our numbers, north or south, east or west.

This brochure explains where census numbers come from and the role those numbers have in the way states and localities redraw the boundaries of their legislative districts. The information here looks in particular at the maps and numbers that state governments and others get from the Census Bureau and use in redistricting.

Chapter 13- This report discusses the constitutionality of legislation, such as the District of Columbia House Voting Rights Act of 2009, H.R. 157 (111th Congress), that would create an at-large congressional district. While it is not without doubt, based on the authority granted to Congress under the Constitution to regulate congressional elections and relevant Supreme Court precedent, it appears that federal law establishing a temporary at-large congressional district would likely be upheld as constitutional.

Chapter 14- In a splintered, complex decision, the U.S. Supreme Court in *League of United Latin American Citizens (LULAC) v. Perry* largely upheld a Texas congressional redistricting plan that was drawn mid-decade against claims of unconstitutional partisan gerrymandering. The Court invalidated one Texas congressional district, District 23, finding that it diluted the voting power of Latinos in violation of Section 2 of the Voting Rights Act. While not ruling out the possibility of a claim of partisan gerrymandering being within

The House of Representatives... ISBN: 978-1-61324-308-4
Editors: R. D. Orsino, O. G. Trance

Chapter 1

THE U.S. HOUSE OF REPRESENTATIVES APPORTIONMENT FORMULA IN THEORY AND PRACTICE*

Royce Crocker

SUMMARY

On December 21, 2010, the number of seats allocated to each state for the House of Representatives was announced. This allocation likely will determine representation to the House for the next five Congresses.

The Constitution requires that states be represented in the House of Representatives in accord with their population. It also requires that each state have at least one Representative, and that there be no more than one Representative for every 30,000 persons. For the 2010 apportionment, this could have meant a House of Representatives as small as 50 or as large as 10,306 Representatives.

Apportioning seats in the House of Representatives among the states in proportion to state population as required by the Constitution appears on the surface to be a simple task. In fact, however, the Constitution presented Congress with issues that provoked extended and recurring debate. How many Representatives should the House comprise? How populous should congressional districts be? What is to be done with the practically inevitable fractional entitlement to a House seat that results

* This is an edited, reformatted and augmented version of a Congressional Research Services publication, dated January 11, 2011.

when the calculations of proportionality are made? How is fairness of apportionment to be best preserved? Apportioning the House can be viewed as a system with four main variables: (1) the size of the House, (2) the population of the states, (3) the number of states, and (4) the method of apportionment.

Over the years since the ratification of the Constitution, the number of Representatives has varied, but in 1941 Congress resolved the issue by fixing the size of the House at 435 members. How to apportion those 435 seats, however, continued to be an issue because of disagreement over how to handle fractional entitlements to a House seat in a way that both met constitutional and statutory requirements and minimized inequity.

The intuitive method of apportionment is to divide the United States population by 435 to obtain an average number of persons represented by a member of the House. This is sometimes called the *ideal size* congressional district. Then a state's population is divided by the ideal size to determine the number of Representatives to be allocated to that state. The quotient will be a whole number plus a remainder—say 14.489326. What is Congress to do with the 0.489326 fractional entitlement? Does the state get 14 or 15 seats in the House? Does one discard the fractional entitlement? Does one round up at the arithmetic mean of the two whole numbers? At the geometric mean? At the harmonic mean? Congress has used, or at least considered, several methods over the years.

Every method Congress has used or considered has its advantages and disadvantages, and none has been exempt from criticism. Under current law, however, seats are apportioned using the equal proportions method, which is not without its critics. Some charge that the equal proportions method is biased toward small states. They urge Congress to adopt either the major fractions or the Hamilton-Vinton method as more equitable alternatives. A strong mathematical case can be made for either equal proportions or major fractions. Deciding between them is a policy matter based on whether minimizing the differences in district sizes in absolute terms (through major fractions) or proportional terms (through equal proportions) is most preferred by Congress.

INTRODUCTION

One of the fundamental issues before the framers at the Constitutional Convention in 1787 was the allocation of representation in Congress between the smaller and larger states.[2] The solution ultimately adopted, known as the Great (or Connecticut) Compromise, resolved the controversy by creating a bicameral Congress with states represented equally in the Senate, but in proportion to population in the House.

The Constitution provided the first apportionment of House seats: 65 Representatives were allocated among the states based on the framers' estimates of how seats might be apportioned following a census.[3] House apportionments thereafter were to be based on Article 1, section 2, as modified by the Fourteenth Amendment:

> *Amendment XIV, section 2.* Representatives shall be apportioned among the several States according to their respective numbers....
>
> *Article 1, section 2.* The number of Representatives shall not exceed one for every thirty Thousand, but each State shall have at least one Representative....

From its beginning in 1789, Congress was faced with questions about how to apportion the House of Representatives—questions that the Constitution did not answer. How populous should a congressional district be on average? How many Representatives should the House comprise? Moreover, no matter how one specified the ideal population of a congressional district or the number of Representatives in the House, a state's ideal apportionment would, as a practical matter, always be either a fraction, or a whole number and a fraction—say, 14.489326. Thus, another question was whether that state would be apportioned 14 or 15 representatives? Consequently, these two major issues dominated the apportionment debate: how populous a congressional district ought to be (later re-cast as how large the House ought to be), and how to treat fractional entitlements to Representatives.[4]

The questions of how populous a congressional district should be and how many Representatives should constitute the House have received little attention since the number of Representatives was last increased from 386 to 435 after the 1910 Census.[5] The problem of fractional entitlement to Representatives, however, continued to be troublesome. Various methods were considered and some were tried, each raising questions of fundamental fairness. The issue of fairness could not be perfectly resolved: inevitable fractional entitlements and the requirement that each state have at least one representative lead to inevitable disparities among the states' average congressional district populations. Congress, which sought an apportionment method that would minimize those disparities, continued this debate until 1941, when it enacted the "equal proportions" method— the apportionment method still in use today (for a full explanation of this method, see below).

In light of the lengthy debate on apportionment, this report has four major purposes:

1) summarize the constitutional and statutory requirements governing apportionment;
2) explain how the current apportionment formula works in theory and in practice;
3) summarize challenges to it on grounds of inequity; and
4) explain the reasoning underlying the choice of the equal proportions method over its chief alternative, the method of major fractions.

CONSTITUTIONAL AND STATUTORY REQUIREMENTS

The process of apportioning seats in the House is constrained both constitutionally and statutorily. As noted previously, the Constitution defines both the maximum and minimum size of the House. There can be no fewer than one Representative per state, and no more than one for every 30,000 persons.[6]

The Apportionment Act of 1941, in addition to specifying the apportionment method, sets the House size at 435, requires an apportionment every 10 years, and mandates administrative procedures for apportionment. The President is required to transmit to Congress "a statement showing the whole number of persons in each state" and the resulting seat allocation within one week after the opening of the first regular session of Congress following the census.[7]

The Census Bureau has been assigned the responsibility of computing the apportionment. As a matter of practice, the Director of the Bureau reports the results of the apportionment at the end of December of the census year. Once received by Congress, the Clerk of the House of Representatives is charged with the duty of sending to the governor of each state a "certificate of the number of Representatives to which such state is entitled" within 15 days of receiving notice from the President.[8]

THE APPORTIONMENT FORMULA

The Formula in Theory

An intuitive way to apportion the House is through simple rounding (a method never adopted by Congress). First, the U.S. apportionment population[9] is divided by the total number of seats in the House (e.g., 309,183,463 divided by 435, in 2010) to identify the "ideal" sized congressional district (708,377 in 2010). Then, each state's population is divided by the "ideal" district population. In most cases this will result in a whole number and a fractional remainder, as noted earlier. Each state will definitely receive seats equal to the whole number, and the fractional remainders will either be rounded up or down (at the .5 "rounding point").

There are two fundamental problems with using simple rounding for apportionment, given a House of fixed size. First, it is possible that some state populations might be so small that they would be "entitled" to less than half a seat. Yet, the Constitution requires that every state must have at least one seat in the House. Thus, a method that relies entirely on rounding will not comply with the Constitution if there are states with very small populations. Second, even a method that assigns each state its constitutional minimum of one seat, and otherwise relies on rounding at the .5 rounding point, might require a "floating" House size because rounding at .5 could result in either fewer or more than 435 seats. Thus, this intuitive way to apportion fails because, by definition, it does not take into account the constitutional requirement that every state have at least one seat in the House and the statutory requirement that the House size be fixed at 435.

The current apportionment method (the method of equal proportions established by the 1941 act) satisfies the constitutional and statutory requirements. Although an equal proportions apportionment is not normally computed in the theoretical way described below, the method can be understood as a modification of the rounding scheme described above.

First, the "ideal" sized district is found (by dividing the apportionment population by 435) to serve as a "trial" divisor.

Then each state's apportionment population is divided by the "ideal" district size to determine its number of seats. Rather than rounding up any remainder of .5 or more, and down for less than .5, however, equal proportions rounds at the geometric mean of any two successive numbers. A geometric mean of two numbers is the square root of the product of the two numbers.[10] If using the "ideal" sized district population as a divisor does not yield 435 seats, the divisor is adjusted upward or downward until rounding at the geometric mean will result in 435 seats.

For example, for the 2010 apportionment, the "ideal" size district of 708,377 had to be adjusted upward to between 709,063 and 710,231[11] to produce a 435-member House. Because the divisor is adjusted so that the total number of seats will equal 435, the problem of the "floating" House size is solved. The constitutional requirement of at least one seat for each state is met by assigning each state one seat automatically regardless of its population size.

The Formula in Practice: Deriving the Apportionment from a Table of "Priority Values"

Although the process of determining an apportionment through a series of trials using divisions near the "ideal" sized district as described above works, it is inefficient because it requires a series of calculations using different divisors until the 435 total is reached. Accordingly, the Census Bureau determines apportionment by computing a "priority" list of state claims to each seat in the House.

During the early 20th century, Walter F. Willcox, a Cornell University mathematician, determined that if the rounding points used in an apportionment method are divided into each state's population (the mathematical equivalent of multiplying the population by the reciprocal of the rounding point), the resulting numbers can be ranked in a priority list for assigning seats in the House.[12]

Such a priority list does not assume a fixed House size because it ranks each of the states' claims to seats in the House so that any size House can be chosen easily without the necessity of extensive re-computations.[13]

The traditional method of constructing a priority list to apportion seats by the equal proportions method involves first computing the reciprocals[14] of the geometric means (the "rounding points") between every pair of consecutive whole numbers (representing the seats to be apportioned). It is then possible to multiply by decimals rather than divide by fractions (the former being a considerably easier task). For example, the reciprocal of the geometric mean between 1 and 2 (1.41452) is 1/1.414452 or .70710678, which becomes the "multiplier" for the priorities for rounding to the second seat for each state. These reciprocals for all pairs (1 to 2, 2 to 3, 3 to 4, etc.) are computed for each "rounding point." They are then used as multipliers to construct the "priority list." *Table 1,* below, provides a list of multipliers used to calculate the "priority values" for each state in an equal proportions apportionment, allowing for the allocation of up to 60 seats to each state.

Table 1. Multipliers for Determining Priority Values for Apportioning the House by the Equal Proportions Method

Seat Assignment	Multiplier[a]	Seat Assignment	Multiplier[a]	Seat Assignment	Multiplier[a]
1	Constitution	21	0.04879500	41	0.02469324
2	0.70710678	22	0.04652421	42	0.02409813
3	0.40824829	23	0.04445542	43	0.02353104
4	0.28867513	24	0.04256283	44	0.02299002
5	0.22360680	25	0.04082483	45	0.02247333
6	0.18257419	26	0.03922323	46	0.02197935
7	0.15430335	27	0.03774257	47	0.02150662
8	0.13363062	28	0.03636965	48	0.02105380
9	0.11785113	29	0.03509312	49	0.02061965
10	0.10540926	30	0.03390318	50	0.02020305
11	0.09534626	31	0.03279129	51	0.01980295
12	0.08703883	32	0.03175003	52	0.01941839
13	0.08006408	33	0.03077287	53	0.01904848
14	0.07412493	34	0.02985407	54	0.01869241
15	0.06900656	35	0.02898855	55	0.01834940
16	0.06454972	36	0.02817181	56	0.01801875
17	0.06063391	37	0.02739983	57	0.01769981
18	0.05716620	38	0.02666904	58	0.01739196
19	0.05407381	39	0.02597622	59	0.01709464
20	0.05129892	40	0.02531848	60	0.01680732

a. Table by CRS, calculated by determining the reciprocal of the geometric mean of successive numbers, $1/\sqrt{n(n-1)}$, where "n" is the number of seats to be allocated to the state.

In order to construct the "priority list," each state's apportionment population is multiplied by each of the multipliers. The resulting products are ranked in order to show each state's claim to seats in the House. For example, (see *Table 2,* below) assume that there are three states in the Union (California, New York, and Florida) and that the House size is set at 30 Representatives. The first seat for each state is assigned by the Constitution; so the remaining 27 seats must be apportioned using the equal proportions formula. The 2010 apportionment populations for these states were 37,341,989 for California, 19,421,055 for New York, and 18,900,773 for Florida.

Once the priority values are computed, they are ranked with the highest value first. The resulting ranking is numbered and seats are assigned until the total is reached. By using the priority rankings instead of the rounding procedures described earlier in this paper under "The Formula in Theory," it is possible to see how an increase or decrease in the House size will affect the allocation of seats without the necessity of additional calculations.

More specifically, for this example in *Table 2,* the computed priority values (column six) for each of the three states are ordered from largest to smallest. By constitutional provision, seats one to three are given to each state. The next determination is the fourth seat in the hypothesized chamber. California's claim to a second seat, based on its priority value, is 26,404,773.64 (0.70710681 x 37,341,989), while New York's claim to a second seat is 13,732,759.69 (0.70710681 x 19,421,055), and Florida's claim to a second seat is 13,364,864.76 (0.70710681 x 18,900,773). Based on the priority values, California has the highest claim for its second seat and is allocated the fourth seat in the hypothesized chamber.

Next, the fifth seat's allocation is determined. California's claim to a third seat, based on the computed priority value, is 15,244,803.17 (0.40824829 x 37,341,989), while, as above, New York's claim to its second seat is 13,732,759.69 (0.70710681 x 19,421,055) and Florida's claim to its second seat is 13,364,864.76 (0.70710681 x 18,900,773). Again, California has a higher priority value, and is allocated its third seat, the fifth seat in the hypothesized chamber.

Table 2. Priority Rankings for Assigning Thirty Seats in a Hypothetical Three-State House Delegation

House Size	State	Seat Assignment	Multiplier (M)	Population (P)	Priority Values (PxM)
4	CA	2	0.707106781	37,341,989	26,404,773.64
5	CA	3	0.40824829	37,341,989	15,244,803.15
6	NY	2	0.707106781	19,421,055	13,732,759.69
7	FL	2	0.707106781	18,900,773	13,364,864.76
8	CA	4	0.288675135	37,341,989	10,779,703.70
9	CA	5	0.223606798	37,341,989	8,349,922.58
10	NY	3	0.40824829	19,421,055	7,928,612.50
11	FL	3	0.40824829	18,900,773	7,716,208.27
12	CA	6	0.182574186	37,341,989	6,817,683.24
13	CA	7	0.15430335	37,341,989	5,761,994.00
14	NY	4	0.288675135	19,421,055	5,606,375.67
15	FL	4	0.288675135	18,900,773	5,456,183.19
16	CA	8	0.133630621	37,341,989	4,990,033.18
17	CA	9	0.11785113	37,341,989	4,400,795.61
18	NY	5	0.223606798	19,421,055	4,342,679.92
19	FL	5	0.223606798	18,900,773	4,226,341.33
20	CA	10	0.105409255	37,341,989	3,936,191.25
21	CA	11	0.095346259	37,341,989	3,560,418.95
22	NY	6	0.18257419	19,421,055	3,545,783.30
23	FL	6	0.182574186	18,900,773	3,450,793.24
24	NY	7	0.15430335	19,421,055	2,996,733.85
25	FL	7	0.15430335	18,900,773	2,916,452.59
26	NY	8	0.133630621	19,421,055	2,595,247.64
27	FL	8	0.133630621	18,900,773	2,525,722.03
28	NY	9	0.11785113	19,421,055	2,288,793.28
29	FL	9	0.11785113	18,900,773	2,227,477.46
30	NY	10	0.10540926	19,421,055	2,047,158.95

Notes: The Constitution requires that each state have at least one seat. Consequently, the first three seats assigned are not included in the table. Table prepared by CRS.

Next the sixth seat's allocation is determined in the same fashion. California's claim to a fourth seat, based on the computed priority value, is 10,779,703.70 (0.288675135 x 37,341,989), while, as above, New York's claim to its second seat is 13,732,759.69 (0.70710681 x 19,421,055) and Florida's claim to its second seat is 13,364,864.76 (0.70710681 x 18,900,773). As New York's priority value is higher than either California's or Florida's, it is allocated its second seat, the sixth seat in the hypothesized chamber.

Next, the seventh seat's allocation is determined. Again, California's claim to a fourth seat, based on the computed priority value, is 10,779,703.70 (0.288675135 x 37,341,989), while, having received its second seat, New York's claim to its third seat is 7,928,612.50(0.40824829 x 19,421,055) and

Florida's claim to its second seat is 13,364,864.76 (0.70710681 x 18,900,773). As Florida's priority value is higher than either of the other states, Florida is, finally, allocated its second seat, the seventh seat in the hypothesized chamber. This same process is continued until all 30 seats in this hypothesized House are allocated to the three states.

From *Table 2,* then, we see that if the United States were made up of three states and the House size were to be set at 30 members, California would have 11 seats, New York would have 10, and Florida would have 9. Any other size House can be determined by picking points in the priority list and observing what the maximum size state delegation size would be for each state.

A priority listing for all 50 states based on the 2010 Census is in the *Appendix* to this report. It shows priority rankings for the assignment of seats in a House ranging in size from 51 to 500 seats.

CHALLENGES TO THE CURRENT FORMULA

The equal proportions rule of rounding at the geometric mean results in differing rounding points, depending on which numbers are chosen. For example, the geometric mean between 1 and 2 is 1.4142, and the geometric mean between 49 and 50 is 49.49747. *Table 3,* below, shows the "rounding points" for assignments to the House using the equal proportions method for a state delegation size of up to 60. The rounding points are listed between each delegation size because they are the thresholds that must be passed in order for a state to be entitled to another seat. The table illustrates that, as the delegation size of a state increases, larger fractions are necessary to entitle the state to additional seats.

The fact that higher rounding points are necessary for states to obtain additional seats has led to charges that the equal proportions formula favors small states at the expense of large states. In *Fair Representation*, a 1982 study of congressional apportionment, authors M.L. Balinski and H.P. Young concluded that if "the intent is to eliminate any systematic advantage to either the small or the large, then only one method, first proposed by Daniel Webster in 1832, will do."[15] This method, called the Webster method in *Fair Representation*, is also referred to as the major fractions method (major fractions uses the concept of the adjustable divisor as does equal proportions, but rounds at the arithmetic mean [.5] rather than the geometric mean.)

Table 3. Rounding Points for Assigning Seats Using the Equal Proportions Method of Apportionment

Size of Delegation	Round Up At	Size of Delegation	Round Up At	Size of Delegation	Round Up At	Size of Delegation	Round Up At
1	1.41421	16	16.49242	31	31.49603	46	46.49731
2	2.44949	17	17.49286	32	32.49615	47	47.49737
3	3.46410	18	18.49324	33	33.49627	48	48.49742
4	4.47214	19	19.49359	34	34.49638	49	49.49747
5	5.47723	20	20.49390	35	35.49648	50	50.49752
6	6.48074	21	21.49419	36	36.49658	51	51.49757
7	7.48331	22	22.49444	37	37.49667	52	52.49762
8	8.48528	23	23.49468	38	38.49675	53	53.49766
9	9.48683	24	24.49490	39	39.49684	54	54.49771
10	10.48809	25	25.49510	40	40.49691	55	55.49775
11	11.48913	26	26.49528	41	41.49699	56	56.49779
12	12.49000	27	27.49545	42	42.49706	57	57.49783
13	13.49074	28	28.49561	43	43.49713	58	58.49786
14	14.49138	29	29.49576	44	44.49719	59	59.49790
15	15.49193	30	30.49590	45	45.49725	60	60.49793

Notes: Any number between 709,063 and 710,231 divided into each state's 2010 population will produce a House size of 435 if rounded at these points, which are the geometric means of each pair of successive numbers. Table prepared by CRS.

Balinski and Young's conclusion in favor of major fractions, however, contradicts a report of the National Academy of Sciences (NAS) prepared at the request of House Speaker Nicholas Longworth in 1929. The NAS concluded that "the method of equal proportions is preferred by the committee because it satisfies ... [certain tests], and because it occupies mathematically a neutral position with respect to emphasis on larger and smaller states."[16]

A bill that would have changed the apportionment method to another formula called the "Hamilton-Vinton" method was introduced in 1981.[17] The fundamental principle of the Hamilton-Vinton method is that it ranks fractional remainders. In order to reapportion the House using Hamilton-Vinton, each state's population would be divided by the "ideal" sized congressional district (309,183,463 divided by 435, in 2010, for an "ideal" district population of 708,377). Any state with fewer residents than the "ideal" sized district would receive a seat because the Constitution requires each state to have at least one House seat. The remaining states in most cases have a claim to a whole number and a fraction of a Representative. Each such state receives the whole number of seats it is entitled to. The fractional remainders are rank-ordered from highest to lowest until 435 seats are assigned. For the purpose of this analysis, we will concentrate on the differences between the equal proportions and major fractions methods because the Hamilton-Vinton method is subject to several mathematical anomalies.[18]

Equal Proportions or Major Fractions: An Analysis

Prior to the passage of the Apportionment Act of 1941 (2 U.S.C. 2(a)), the two contending methods considered by Congress were the equal proportions method (Hill-Huntington) and the method of major fractions (Webster). Each of the major competing methods—equal proportions (currently used) and major fractions—can be supported mathematically. Choosing between them is a policy decision, rather than a matter of conclusively proving that one approach is mathematically better than the other. A major fractions apportionment results in a House in which each citizen's share of his or her Representative is as equal as possible on an absolute basis. In the equal proportions apportionment now used, each citizen's share of his or her Representative is as equal as possible on a proportional basis. From a policy standpoint, a case can be made for either method of computing the apportionment of seats by arguing that one measure of fairness is preferable to the other.

The Case for Major Fractions

As noted above, a major fractions apportionment results in a House in which each person's share of his or her Representative is as equal as possible on an absolute basis. As an example, in 2010, the state of North Carolina would have been assigned 14 seats under the major fractions method, and the state of Rhode Island would have received 1 seat. Under this allocation, there would have been 1.4636 Representatives per million for North Carolina residents and 0.9476 Representatives per million for Rhode Island residents. The absolute value[19] of the difference between these two numbers is 0.5160.

Under the equal proportion method of assigning seats in 2010, North Carolina actually received 13 seats and Rhode Island 2. With 13 seats, North Carolina received 1.3590 Representatives for each million persons, and Rhode Island, with 2 seats, received 1.8953 Representatives per million persons. The absolute value of the difference between these two numbers is 0.5363. As this example shows, using the major fractions method produces a difference in the share of a Representative between the states that is smaller, in an absolute sense, than is the difference produced by the equal proportions method.

In addition, it can be argued that the major fractions minimization of absolute size differences among districts more closely reflects the "one person, one vote" principle established by the Supreme Court in its series of redistricting cases (*Baker* v. *Carr*, 369 U.S. 186 (1964) through *Karcher* v. *Daggett*, 462 U.S.725 (1983).[20]

Although the "one person, one vote" rules have not been applied by the courts to apportioning seats *among* states, the method of major fractions can reduce the range between the smallest and largest district sizes more than the method of equal proportions—one of the measures that the courts have applied to within-state redistricting cases. Although this range would have not changed in 2000 or 1990, if the method of major fractions had been used in 1980, the smallest average district size in the country would have been 399,592 (one of Nevada's two districts). With the method of equal proportions it was 393,345 (one of Montana's two districts). In both cases the largest district was 690,178 (South Dakota's single seat).[21] Thus, in 1980, shifting from equal proportions to major fractions as a method of apportionment would have improved the 296,833 difference between the largest and smallest districts by 6,247 persons.

It can be argued, because the equal proportions rounding points ascend as the number of seats increases, rather than staying at .5, that small states may be favored in seat assignments at the expense of large states. It is possible to demonstrate this by using simulation techniques.

The House has been reapportioned only 21 times since 1790. The equal proportions method has been used in five apportionments, and the major fractions method in three. Eight apportionments do not provide sufficient historical information to enable policy makers to generalize about the impact of using differing methods. Computers, however, can enable reality to be simulated by using random numbers to test many different hypothetical situations. These techniques (such as the "Monte Carlo" simulation method) are a useful way to observe the behavior of systems when experience does not provide sufficient information to generalize about them.

Apportioning the House can be viewed as a system with four main variables: (1) the size of the House, (2) the population of the states,[22] (3) the number of states,[23] and (4) the method of apportionment.[24] A 1984 exercise prepared for the Congressional Research Service (CRS) involving 1,000 simulated apportionments examined the results when two of these variables were changed—the method and the state populations. In order to further approximate reality, the state populations used in the apportionments were based on the Census Bureau's 1990 population projections available at that time. Each method was tested by computing 1,000 apportionments and tabulating the results by state. There was no discernible pattern by size of state in the results of the major fractions apportionment. The equal proportions exercise, however, showed that the smaller states were persistently advantaged.[25]

Another way of evaluating the impact of a possible change in apportionment methods is to determine the odds of an outcome being different than the one produced by the current method— equal proportions. If equal proportions favors small states at the expense of large states, would switching to major fractions, a method that appears not to be influenced by the size of a state, increase the odds of the large states gaining additional representation? Based on the simulation model prepared for CRS, this appears to be true. The odds of any of the 23 largest states gaining an additional seat in any given apportionment range from a maximum of 13.4% of the time (California) to a low of .2% of the time (Alabama). The odds of any of the 21 multi-districted smaller states losing a seat range from a high of 17% (Montana, which then had two seats) to a low of 0% (Colorado), if major fractions were used instead of equal proportions.

In the aggregate, switching from equal proportions to major fractions "could be expected to shift zero seats about 37% of the time, to shift 1 seat about 49% of the time, 2 seats 12% of the time, and 3 seats 2% of the time (and 4 or more seats almost never), and, these shifts will always be from smaller states to larger states."[26]

In summary, then, the method of major fractions minimizes the absolute differences in the share of a representative between congressional districts across states. In addition, it appears that the method of major fractions does not favor large or small states over the long term.

The Case for Equal Proportions, the Current Method

Support for the equal proportions formula primarily rests on the belief that minimizing the proportional differences among districts is more important than minimizing the absolute differences. Laurence Schmeckebier, a proponent of the equal proportions method, wrote in *Congressional Apportionment* in 1941, that

> Mathematicians generally agree that the significant feature of a difference is its relation to the smaller number and not its absolute quantity. Thus the increase of 50 horsepower in the output of two engines would not be of any significance if one engine already yielded 10,000 horsepower, but it would double the efficiency of a plant of only 50 horsepower. It has been shown ... that the relative difference between two apportionments is always least if the method of equal proportions is used. Moreover, the method of equal proportions is the only one that uses relative differences, the methods of harmonic mean and major fraction being based on absolute differences. In addition, the method of equal proportions gives the smallest relative difference for both average population per district and individual share in a representative. No other method takes account of both these factors. Therefore the method of equal proportions gives the most equitable distribution of Representatives among the states.[27]

An example using the North Carolina and Rhode Island 2010 populations illustrates the argument for proportional differences. The first step in making comparisons between the states is to standardize the figures in some fashion. One way of doing this is to express each state's representation in the House as a number of Representatives per million residents.[28] The equal proportions formula assigned 13 seats to North Carolina and 2 to Rhode Island in 2010. If the major fractions method had been used, then 14 seats would have been assigned to North Carolina, and 1 would have been given to Rhode Island. Under this scenario, North Carolina has 1.4636 Representatives per million persons and Rhode Island has 0.9476 Representatives per million. The absolute difference between these numbers is 0.5160 and the proportional difference between the two states' Representatives per million is 54.45%. When 13 seats are assigned to North Carolina and 2 are assigned to Rhode Island (using equal proportions), North Carolina has 1.3590 Representatives per million and Rhode Island has 1.8953 Representatives per million. The absolute difference between these numbers is .0.5363 and the proportional difference is 39.46%.

Major fractions minimizes absolute differences, so in 2010, if this method had been required by law, North Carolina and Rhode Island would have received 14 and 1 seats respectively because the absolute difference (0.5160 Representatives per million) is smaller at 14 and 1 than it would be at 13 and 2 (0.5363). Equal proportions minimizes differences on a proportional basis, so it assigned 13 seats to North Carolina and 2 to Rhode Island because the proportional difference between a 13 and 2 allocation (39.46%) is smaller than would occur with a 14 and 1 assignment (54.45%).

The proportional difference versus absolute difference argument could also be cast in terms of the goal of "one person, one vote," as noted above. The courts' use of absolute difference measures in state redistricting cases may not necessarily be appropriate when applied to the apportionment of seats among states. The courts already recognize that the rules governing redistricting in state legislatures differ from those in congressional districting. If the "one person, one vote" standard were ever to be applied to apportionment of seats among states—a process that differs significantly from redistricting within states—proportional difference measures might be accepted as most appropriate.[29]

If the choice between methods were judged to be a tossup with regard to which mathematical process is fairest, are there other representational goals that equal proportions meets that are, perhaps, appropriate to consider? One such goal might be the desirability of avoiding large districts, if possible. After the apportionment of 2010, five of the seven states with only one Representative (Alaska, Delaware, Montana, North Dakota, South Dakota, Vermont, and Wyoming) have relatively large land areas.[30] The five Representatives of the larger states will serve 1.22% of the U.S. population, but also will represent 27% of the U.S. total land area.

Arguably, an apportionment method that would potentially reduce the number of very large districts would serve to increase representation in those states. Very large districts limit the opportunities of constituents to see their Representatives, may require more district based offices, and may require toll calls for telephone contact with the Representatives' district offices. Switching from equal proportions to major fractions may increase the number of states represented by only one member of Congress, although it is impossible to predict this outcome with any certainty using Census Bureau projections for 2025.[31]

The table that follows contains the priority listing used in apportionment following the 2010 Census. **Table A-1** shows where each state ranked in the priority of seat assignments. The priority values listed beyond seat number 435 show which states would have gained additional representations if the House size had been increased.

APPENDIX. 2010 PRIORITY LIST FOR APPORTIONING SEATS TO THE HOUSE OF REPRESENTATIVES

Table A-1. 2010 Priority List for Apportioning Seats to the House of Representatives

Seat Sequence	State	Seat Number	Priority Value
51	California	2	26,404,773.64
52	Texas	2	17,867,469.72
53	California	3	15,244,803.17
54	New York	2	13,732,759.69
55	Florida	2	13,364,864.76
56	California	4	10,779,703.70
57	Texas	3	10,315,788.45
58	Illinois	2	9,096,490.33
59	Pennsylvania	2	9,004,937.68
60	California	5	8,349,922.58
61	Ohio	2	8,180,161.26
62	New York	3	7,928,612.50
63	Florida	3	7,716,208.27
64	Texas	4	7,294,363.97
65	Michigan	2	7,008,577.96
66	Georgia	2	6,878,427.88
67	California	6	6,817,683.24
68	North Carolina	2	6,764,028.61
69	New Jersey	2	6,227,843.68

Table A-1. (Continued).

Seat Sequence	State	Seat Number	Priority Value
70	California	7	5,761,994.00
71	Virginia	2	5,683,537.63
72	Texas	5	5,650,190.03
73	New York	4	5,606,375.67
74	Florida	4	5,456,183.19
75	Illinois	3	5,251,861.14
76	Pennsylvania	3	5,199,003.20
77	California	8	4,990,033.18
78	Washington	2	4,775,353.02
79	Ohio	3	4,722,818.31
80	Massachusetts	2	4,638,368.75
81	Texas	6	4,613,360.84
82	Indiana	2	4,597,312.72
83	Arizona	2	4,534,463.66
84	Tennessee	2	4,508,110.49
85	California	9	4,400,795.61
86	New York	5	4,342,679.92
87	Missouri	2	4,250,756.86
88	Florida	5	4,226,341.33
89	Maryland	2	4,094,098.06
90	Michigan	3	4,046,404.37
91	Wisconsin	2	4,029,257.07
92	Georgia	3	3,971,262.19
93	California	10	3,936,191.25
94	North Carolina	3	3,905,213.74
95	Texas	7	3,899,001.55
96	Minnesota	2	3,758,186.98
97	Illinois	4	3,713,626.63
98	Pennsylvania	4	3,676,250.41
99	New Jersey	3	3,595,647.23
100	Colorado	2	3,567,304.21
101	California	11	3,560,418.95
102	New York	6	3,545,783.30
103	Florida	6	3,450,793.24
104	Alabama	2	3,396,221.14
105	Texas	8	3,376,634.39
106	Ohio	4	3,339,536.85
107	South Carolina	2	3,285,200.43
108	Virginia	3	3,281,391.98
109	California	12	3,250,202.96
110	Louisiana	2	3,220,137.41
111	Kentucky	2	3,076,343.00
112	New York	7	2,996,733.85

Seat Sequence	State	Seat Number	Priority Value
113	California	13	2,989,751.88
114	Texas	9	2,977,911.62
115	Florida	7	2,916,452.59
116	Illinois	5	2,876,562.82
117	Michigan	4	2,861,239.97
118	Pennsylvania	5	2,847,611.33
119	Georgia	4	2,808,106.42
120	California	14	2,767,972.38
121	North Carolina	4	2,761,403.12
122	Washington	3	2,757,051.35
123	Oregon	2	2,721,375.40
124	Massachusetts	3	2,677,963.45
125	Texas	10	2,663,525.12
126	Oklahoma	2	2,662,173.59
127	Indiana	3	2,654,259.74
128	Arizona	3	2,617,973.81
129	Tennessee	3	2,602,758.81
130	New York	8	2,595,247.64
131	Ohio	5	2,586,794.12
132	California	15	2,576,842.05
133	New Jersey	4	2,542,506.54
134	Connecticut	2	2,532,593.45
135	Florida	8	2,525,722.03
136	Missouri	3	2,454,175.62
137	California	16	2,410,415.03
138	Texas	11	2,409,249.13
139	Maryland	3	2,363,728.62
140	Illinois	6	2,348,703.70
141	Wisconsin	3	2,326,292.66
142	Pennsylvania	6	2,325,064.91
143	Virginia	4	2,320,294.52
144	New York	9	2,288,793.28
145	California	17	2,264,190.66
146	Florida	9	2,227,477.46
147	Michigan	5	2,216,306.95
148	Texas	12	2,199,333.49
149	Georgia	5	2,175,149.88
150	Minnesota	3	2,169,790.27
151	Iowa	2	2,159,353.50
152	North Carolina	5	2,138,973.66
153	California	18	2,134,699.43
154	Ohio	6	2,112,108.56
155	Mississippi	2	2,105,933.70
156	Arkansas	2	2,069,156.37
157	Colorado	3	2,059,584.05
158	New York	10	2,047,158.95

Table A-1. (Continued).

Seat Sequence	State	Seat Number	Priority Value
159	Kansas	2	2,025,021.59
160	Texas	13	2,023,092.56
161	California	19	2,019,223.51
162	Florida	10	1,992,316.41
163	Illinois	7	1,985,016.93
164	New Jersey	5	1,969,417.09
165	Pennsylvania	7	1,965,038.50
166	Alabama	3	1,960,809.19
167	Utah	2	1,959,226.72
168	Washington	4	1,949,529.71
169	Nevada	2	1,915,857.74
170	California	20	1,915,603.62
171	South Carolina	3	1,896,711.35
172	Massachusetts	4	1,893,606.11
173	Indiana	4	1,876,845.06
174	Texas	14	1,873,019.76
175	Louisiana	3	1,859,147.20
176	New York	11	1,851,724.94
177	Arizona	4	1,851,187.04
178	Tennessee	4	1,840,428.40
179	California	21	1,822,102.49
180	Michigan	6	1,809,607.05
181	Florida	11	1,802,118.00
182	Virginia	5	1,797,292.41
183	Ohio	7	1,785,057.53
184	Kentucky	3	1,776,127.46
185	Georgia	6	1,776,002.44
186	North Carolina	6	1,746,464.68
187	Texas	15	1,743,686.50
188	California	22	1,737,306.56
189	Missouri	4	1,735,364.22
190	Illinois	8	1,719,075.09
191	Pennsylvania	8	1,701,773.26
192	New York	12	1,690,385.87
193	Maryland	4	1,671,408.53
194	California	23	1,660,053.90
195	Florida	12	1,645,101.13
196	Wisconsin	4	1,644,937.31
197	Texas	16	1,631,069.37
198	New Jersey	6	1,608,022.32
199	California	24	1,589,380.60
200	Oregon	3	1,571,186.82
201	New York	13	1,554,928.84
202	Ohio	8	1,545,905.17

Seat Sequence	State	Seat Number	Priority Value
203	Oklahoma	3	1,537,006.64
204	Minnesota	4	1,534,273.41
205	Texas	17	1,532,122.89
206	Michigan	7	1,529,397.10
207	California	25	1,524,480.32
208	Illinois	9	1,516,081.72
209	Florida	13	1,513,272.94
210	Washington	5	1,510,099.22
211	Georgia	7	1,500,996.02
212	Pennsylvania	9	1,500,822.95
213	North Carolina	7	1,476,032.05
214	Virginia	6	1,467,483.11
215	Massachusetts	5	1,466,780.99
216	California	26	1,464,673.31
217	Connecticut	3	1,462,193.51
218	New Mexico	2	1,461,782.76
219	Colorado	4	1,456,345.85
220	Indiana	5	1,453,797.93
221	Texas	18	1,444,499.31
222	New York	14	1,439,584.37
223	Arizona	5	1,433,923.31
224	Tennessee	5	1,425,589.71
225	California	27	1,409,382.55
226	Florida	14	1,401,018.51
227	Alabama	4	1,386,501.48
228	Texas	19	1,366,359.56
229	Ohio	9	1,363,360.21
230	New Jersey	7	1,359,026.91
231	California	28	1,358,115.01
232	Illinois	10	1,356,024.72
233	Missouri	5	1,344,207.35
234	Pennsylvania	10	1,342,376.85
235	South Carolina	4	1,341,177.46
236	New York	15	1,340,180.12
237	Michigan	8	1,324,496.74
238	West Virginia	2	1,315,087.80
239	Louisiana	4	1,314,615.59
240	California	29	1,310,446.91
241	Florida	15	1,304,277.25
242	Georgia	8	1,299,900.68
243	Texas	20	1,296,242.49
244	Nebraska	2	1,295,295.88
245	Maryland	5	1,294,667.48
246	North Carolina	8	1,278,281.25
247	Wisconsin	5	1,274,162.96
248	California	30	1,266,011.99
249	Kentucky	4	1,255,911.77

Table A-1. (Continued).

Seat Sequence	State	Seat Number	Priority Value
250	New York	16	1,253,623.71
251	Iowa	3	1,246,703.32
252	Virginia	7	1,240,249.59
253	Washington	6	1,232,990.85
254	Texas	21	1,232,972.55
255	Illinois	11	1,226,570.51
256	California	31	1,224,492.06
257	Florida	16	1,220,039.65
258	Ohio	10	1,219,426.44
259	Mississippi	3	1,215,861.39
260	Pennsylvania	11	1,214,225.55
261	Massachusetts	6	1,197,621.66
262	Arkansas	3	1,194,627.99
263	Minnesota	5	1,188,443.07
264	Indiana	6	1,187,021.04
265	California	32	1,185,609.34
266	New York	17	1,177,574.43
267	New Jersey	8	1,176,951.83
268	Texas	22	1,175,593.20
269	Arizona	6	1,170,793.48
270	Kansas	3	1,169,146.76
271	Michigan	9	1,168,096.33
272	Tennessee	6	1,163,989.12
273	California	33	1,149,120.28
274	Georgia	9	1,146,404.65
275	Florida	17	1,146,027.70
276	Utah	3	1,131,160.07
277	Colorado	5	1,128,080.64
278	North Carolina	9	1,127,338.10
279	Texas	23	1,123,318.20
280	Illinois	12	1,119,700.56
281	California	34	1,114,810.42
282	Idaho	2	1,112,631.81
283	Oregon	4	1,110,996.86
284	New York	18	1,110,227.82
285	Pennsylvania	12	1,108,431.21
286	Nevada	3	1,106,120.98
287	Ohio	11	1,103,012.72
288	Missouri	6	1,097,540.70
289	Oklahoma	4	1,086,827.82
290	California	35	1,082,490.18
291	Florida	18	1,080,485.28
292	Texas	24	1,075,495.29
293	Virginia	8	1,074,087.65

294	Alabama	5	1,073,979.42
295	Maryland	6	1,057,091.57
296	California	36	1,051,991.36
297	New York	19	1,050,170.38
298	Michigan	10	1,044,777.12
299	Washington	7	1,042,067.46
300	Wisconsin	6	1,040,349.70
301	South Carolina	5	1,038,871.59
302	New Jersey	9	1,037,973.95
303	Connecticut	4	1,033,926.94
304	Texas	25	1,031,578.85
305	Illinois	13	1,029,974.71
306	Georgia	10	1,025,375.49
307	California	37	1,023,164.20
308	Florida	19	1,022,036.75
309	Pennsylvania	13	1,019,608.41
310	Louisiana	5	1,018,296.86
311	Massachusetts	7	1,012,175.04
312	North Carolina	10	1,008,321.85
313	Ohio	12	1,006,908.25
314	Indiana	7	1,003,215.88
315	New York	20	996,279.10
316	California	38	995,874.90
317	Texas	26	991,108.90
318	Arizona	7	989,501.09
319	Tennessee	7	983,750.36
320	Kentucky	5	972,825.08
321	Minnesota	6	970,359.71
322	California	39	970,003.60
323	Florida	20	969,589.20
324	Hawaii	2	966,517.39
325	Texas	27	953,694.98
326	Illinois	14	953,571.29
327	New York	21	947,650.45
328	Virginia	9	947,256.27
329	California	40	945,442.56
330	Michigan	11	945,036.46
331	Pennsylvania	14	943,973.96
332	Maine	2	942,625.67
333	New Hampshire	2	934,402.72
334	New Jersey	10	928,392.12
335	Missouri	7	927,591.19
336	Georgia	11	927,487.03
337	Ohio	13	926,220.87
338	Florida	21	922,263.29
339	California	41	922,094.69
340	Colorado	6	921,073.99
341	Texas	28	919,003.48
342	North Carolina	11	912,061.43

Table A-1. (Continued).

Seat Sequence	State	Seat Number	Priority Value
343	New York	22	903,549.25
344	Washington	8	902,456.89
345	California	42	899,872.28
346	Maryland	7	893,405.44
347	Illinois	15	887,726.56
348	Texas	29	886,747.63
349	Iowa	4	881,552.37
350	Florida	22	879,343.54
351	Wisconsin	7	879,255.98
352	Pennsylvania	15	878,791.93
353	California	43	878,695.85
354	Alabama	6	876,900.53
355	Massachusetts	8	876,569.30
356	Indiana	8	868,810.44
357	New York	23	863,371.20
358	Michigan	12	862,696.31
359	Oregon	5	860,574.46
360	Mississippi	4	859,743.83
361	California	44	858,493.24
362	Ohio	14	857,513.90
363	Arizona	8	856,933.08
364	Texas	30	856,679.60
365	Tennessee	8	851,952.80
366	South Carolina	6	848,235.10
367	Virginia	10	847,251.77
368	Georgia	12	846,675.94
369	Arkansas	4	844,729.55
370	New Mexico	3	843,960.67
371	Oklahoma	5	841,853.21
372	Florida	23	840,241.85
373	New Jersey	11	839,762.27
374	California	45	839,198.79
375	North Carolina	12	832,594.37
376	Louisiana	6	831,435.90
377	Illinois	16	830,392.16
378	Texas	31	828,584.07
379	Kansas	4	826,711.60
380	New York	24	826,615.00
381	Pennsylvania	16	822,034.58
382	California	46	820,752.61
383	Minnesota	7	820,103.63
384	Florida	24	804,470.32
385	Missouri	8	803,317.54
386	California	47	803,099.96

387	Texas	32	802,273.07
388	Connecticut	5	800,876.37
389	Utah	4	799,850.96
390	Ohio	15	798,302.00
391	Washington	9	795,892.17
392	Kentucky	6	794,308.35
393	Michigan	13	793,565.19
394	New York	25	792,861.25
395	California	48	786,190.69
396	Nevada	4	782,145.65
397	Illinois	17	780,017.61
398	Georgia	13	778,828.59
399	Colorado	7	778,449.60
400	Texas	33	777,581.81
401	Maryland	8	773,711.81
402	Massachusetts	9	773,061.46
403	Pennsylvania	17	772,167.04
404	Florida	25	771,620.83
405	California	49	769,978.84
406	New Jersey	12	766,594.56
407	Virginia	11	766,368.06
408	Indiana	9	766,218.79
409	North Carolina	13	765,875.43
410	New York	26	761,756.45
411	Wisconsin	8	761,458.01
412	West Virginia	3	759,266.29
413	Arizona	9	755,743.94
414	California	50	754,422.10
415	Texas	34	754,365.16
416	Tennessee	9	751,351.75
417	Nebraska	3	747,839.42
418	Ohio	16	746,743.14
419	Rhode Island	2	746,172.31
420	Florida	26	741,349.31
421	Alabama	7	741,116.21
422	California	51	739,481.57
423	Illinois	18	735,407.66
424	Michigan	14	734,698.60
425	New York	27	733,000.49
426	Texas	35	732,494.84
427	Pennsylvania	18	728,006.06
428	California	52	725,121.34
429	Georgia	14	721,055.17
430	South Carolina	7	716,889.51
431	Florida	27	713,363.71
432	Washington	10	711,867.60

Table A-1. (Continued).

Seat Sequence	State	Seat Number	Priority Value
433	Texas	36	711,857.03
434	California	53	711,308.24
435	Minnesota	8	710,230.58
	Last seat assigned by current law		
436	North Carolina	14	709,062.86
437	Missouri	9	708,459.48
438	New York	28	706,336.94
439	New Jersey	13	705,164.44
440	Montana	2	703,158.30
441	Louisiana	7	702,691.59
442	Oregon	6	702,656.11
443	Ohio	17	701,443.04
444	Virginia	12	699,595.12
445	California	54	698,011.59
446	Illinois	19	695,626.00
447	Texas	37	692,350.39
448	Massachusetts	10	691,447.19
449	Pennsylvania	19	688,624.80
450	Florida	28	687,414.47
451	Oklahoma	6	687,370.27
452	Indiana	10	685,326.92
453	California	55	685,202.95
454	Michigan	15	683,967.17
455	Iowa	5	682,847.53
456	Maryland	9	682,349.68
457	New York	29	681,545.42
458	Arizona	10	675,957.93
459	Colorado	8	674,157.13
460	Texas	38	673,884.38
461	California	56	672,855.94
462	Tennessee	10	672,029.43
463	Wisconsin	9	671,542.85
464	Kentucky	7	671,313.08
465	Georgia	15	671,265.83
466	Mississippi	5	665,954.71
467	Florida	29	663,287.10
468	Ohio	18	661,326.84
469	California	57	660,946.04
470	North Carolina	15	660,101.60
471	Illinois	20	659,928.77
472	New York	30	658,435.43
473	Texas	39	656,377.90
474	Arkansas	5	654,324.70
475	Connecticut	6	653,912.82

476	Pennsylvania	20	653,286.84
477	New Jersey	14	652,855.41
478	California	58	649,450.45
479	Washington	11	643,908.47
480	Virginia	13	643,533.91
481	Idaho	3	642,378.28
482	Alabama	8	641,825.47
483	Florida	30	640,796.22
484	Kansas	5	640,368.05
485	Michigan	16	639,792.71
486	Texas	40	639,758.04
487	California	59	638,347.91
488	Delaware	2	637,016.24
489	New York	31	636,841.48
490	Missouri	10	633,665.42
491	Georgia	16	627,911.69
492	Illinois	21	627,717.47
493	California	60	627,618.61
494	Minnesota	9	626,364.50
495	Ohio	19	625,552.57
496	Massachusetts	11	625,437.52
497	Texas	41	623,959.11
498	Pennsylvania	21	621,399.74
499	South Carolina	8	620,844.52
500	Indiana	11	619,901.52

Notes: Prepared by CRS.

End Notes

[1] A similar, previous CRS report was authored by David C. Huckabee, who retired in 2005. While the current report is modified by the current author, Mr. Huckabee's contribution, in a large part, remains. Of course, any errors that may appear are due solely to the current author.

[2] In part, this debate over the apportionment of power in the early years of this country came from the 10-year experience with the unicameral congress provided for under the Articles of Confederation, which assigned one vote to each state delegation in Congress. For a thorough discussion, see Charles A. Kromkowski, *Recreating the American Republic*, (Cambridge University Press, Cambridge, U.K., 2002), esp., pp. 261-307.

[3] A major controversy occurred even over the fixed, short-term apportionment of seats among the delegates at the Constitutional Convention. See Kromkowski, pp. 287-294.

[4] Thomas Jefferson recommended discarding the fractions. Daniel Webster and others argued that Jefferson's method was unconstitutional because it discriminated against small states. Webster argued that an additional Representative should be awarded to a state if the fractional entitlement was 0.5 or greater—a method that decreased the size of the house by 17 members in 1832. Congress subsequently used a "fixed ratio" method proposed by Rep. Samuel Vinton following the census of 1850 through 1900, but this method led to the

paradox that Alabama lost a seat even though the size of the House was increased in 1880. Subsequently, mathematician W.F. Willcox proposed the "major fractions" method, which was used following the census of 1910. This method, too, had its critics; and in 1921 Harvard mathematician E.V. Huntington proposed the "equal proportions" method and developed formulas and computational tables for all of the other known, mathematically valid apportionment methods. A committee of the National Academy of Sciences conducted an analysis of each of those methods—smallest divisors, harmonic mean, equal proportions, major fractions, and greatest divisors—and recommended that Congress adopt Huntington's equal proportions method. For a review of this history, see U.S. Congress, House, Committee on Post Office and Civil Service, Subcommittee on Census and Statistics, *The Decennial Population Census and Congressional Apportionment*, 91st Congress, 2nd session. H. Report 91-1314 (Washington: GPO, 1970), Appendix B, pp. 15-18. Also, see Michel L. Balinski and H. Peyton Young, *Fair Representation*, 2nd edition, (Brookings Institution Press, Washington, 2001).

5 Article I, Section 2 defines both the maximum and minimum size of the House, but the actual House size is set by law. There can be no fewer than one Representative per state, and no more than one for every 30,000 persons. Thus, the House after 2010 could be as small as 50 and as large as 10,306 Representatives.

6 The actual language in of Article 1, section 2 pertaining to this minimum size reads as follows: "The number of Representatives shall not exceed one for every thirty Thousand, but each State shall have at least one Representative." This clause is sometime misread to be a requirement that districts can be no larger than 30,000 persons, rather than as it should be read, as a minimum-size population requirement.

7 55 Stat. 761. (1941) Sec. 22 (a). [Codified in 2 U.S.C. 2(a).] In other words, after the 2010 Census, this report is due in January 2010. Interestingly, while the Constitution requires a census every ten years, it does not require that an apportionment of seats to the House of Representatives must occur. This became a statutory requirement with the passage of the Apportionment Act of 1941.

8 Ibid., Sec. 22 (b).

9 The apportionment population is the resident population of the 50 states. It excludes the population of the District of Columbia and U.S. territories and possessions, but since 1970, excepting 1980, it has included the overseas federal and military employees and their families.

10 The geometric mean of 1 and 2 is the square root of 2, which is 1.4142. The geometric mean of 2 and 3 is the square root of 6, which is 2.4495. Geometric means are computed for determining the rounding points for the size of any state's delegation size. Equal proportions rounds at the geometric mean (which varies) rather than the arithmetic mean (which is always halfway between any pair of numbers). Thus, a state which would be entitled to 10.4871 seats before rounding will be rounded down to 10 because the geometric mean of 10 and 11 is 10.4881. The rationale for choosing the geometric mean rather than the arithmetic mean as the rounding point is discussed below in the section analyzing the equal proportions and major fractions formulas.

11 Any number in this range divided into each state's population and rounded at the geometric mean will produce a 435- seat House, with the provision that each state receives at least one seat.

12 U.S. Congress, House Committee on Post Office and Civil Service, Subcommittee on the Census and Statistics, *The Decennial Population Census and Congressional Apportionment*, 91st Congress, 2nd session, H. Report 91-1814, (Washington: GPO, 1970), p. 16.

[13] The 435 limit on the size of the House is a statutory requirement. The House size was first fixed at 435 by the Apportionment Act of 1911 (37 Stat. 13). The Apportionment Act of 1929 (46 Stat. 26), as amended by the Apportionment Act of 1941 (54 Stat. 162), provided for "automatic reapportionment" rather than requiring the Congress to pass a new apportionment law each decade. This requirement to "automatically reapportion" every 10 years was needed because the Constitution, ironically, while requiring a census every 10 years makes no such requirement for apportionments. Thus, the fact that no apportionment was carried out after the 1920 census in no way violated the Constitution or any statutory requirement at the time. By authority of section 9 of PL 85-508 (72 Stat. 345) and section 8 of PL 86-3 (73 Stat. 8), which admitted Alaska and Hawaii to statehood, the House size was temporarily increased to 437 until the reapportionment resulting from the 1960 Census when it returned to 435.

[14] A reciprocal of a number is that number divided into one.

[15] *Fair Representation*, pp. 3-4. (An earlier major work in this field was written by Laurence F. Schmeckebier, *Congressional Apportionment* (Washington: The Brookings Institution, 1941). Daniel Webster proposed this method to overcome the large-state bias in Jefferson's discarded fractions method. Webster's method was used three times, in the reapportionments following the 1840, 1910, and 1930 Censuses.

[16] "Report of the National Academy of Sciences Committee on Apportionment" in *The Decennial Population Census and Congressional Apportionment*, Appendix C, p. 21.

[17] H.R. 1990, 97th Congress was introduced by Representative Floyd Fithian and was cosponsored by 10 other members of the Indiana delegation. Changing to the Hamilton-Vinton method would have kept Indiana from losing a seat. Hearings were held, but no further action was taken on the measure. U.S. Congress, House Committee on Post Office and Civil Service, Subcommittee on Census and Population, *Census Activities and the Decennial Census*, hearing, 97th Cong., 1st sess., June 11, 1981, (Washington: GPO, 1981). Since that time no other bill has been introduced to change the formula.

[18] The Hamilton-Vinton method (used after the 1850-1900 censuses) is subject to the "Alabama paradox" and various other population paradoxes. The Alabama paradox was so named in 1880 when it was discovered that Alabama would have lost a seat in the House if the size of the House had been increased from 299 to 300. Another paradox, known as the population paradox, has been variously described, but in its modern form (with a fixed size House) it works in this way: two states may gain population from one census to the next. State "A," which is gaining population at a rate faster than state "B," may lose a seat to state "B." There are other paradoxes of this type. Hamilton-Vinton is subject to them, whereas equal proportions and major fractions are not.

[19] The absolute value of a number is its magnitude without regard to its sign. For example, the absolute value of -8 is 8. The absolute value of the expression (4-2) is 2. The absolute value of the expression (2-4) is also 2.

[20] Major fractions best conforms to the spirit of these decisions if the population discrepancy is measured on an absolute basis, as the courts have done in the recent past. The Supreme Court has never applied its "one person, one vote" rule to apportioning seats of the House of Representatives among states (as opposed to redistricting within states). Thus, no established rule of law is being violated. Arguably, no apportionment method can meet the "one person, one vote" standard required by the Supreme Court for districts within states unless the size of the House is increased significantly (thereby making districts less populous).

[21] Nevada had two seats with a population of 799,184. Montana was assigned two seats with a population of 786,690. South Dakota's single seat was required by the Constitution (with a population of 690,178). The vast majority of the districts based on the 1980 census (323 of them) fell within the range of 501,000 to 530,000).

[22] For varying the definition of the population, see CRS Report RS22124, *Potential House Apportionment Following the 2010 Census Based on Census Bureau Population Projections*, by Royce Crocker, and, Royce Crocker, *Apportioning Representatives Among States by Citizen Populations Instead of Total State Populations,* CRS Congressional Distribution Memorandum, May 8, 2007.

[23] For information on the impact of adding states, see CRS Report RS22579, *District of Columbia Representation: Effect on House Apportionment*, by Royce Crocker, and CRS Report R41113, *Puerto Rican Statehood: Effects on House Apportionment*, by Royce Crocker.

[24] See CRS Archived CRS Report RL31074, *The House of Representatives Apportionment Formula: An Analysis of Proposals for Change and Their Impact on States*, by Royce Crocker.

[25] H.P. Young and M.L. Balinski, *Evaluation of Apportionment Methods*, Prepared under a contract for the Congressional Research Service of the Library of Congress. (Contract No. CRS84-15), Sept. 30, 1984, available to members of Congress and congressional staff from the author of this report. Comparing equal proportions and major fractions using the state populations from the 19 actual censuses taken since 1790, reveals that the small states would have been favored 3.4% of the time if equal proportions had been used for all the apportionments. Major fractions would have also favored small states, in these cases, but only .06 % of the time. See *Fair Representation*, p. 78.

[26] Young and Balinski, *Evaluation of Apportionment Methods*, p. 13.

[27] Schmeckebier, *Congressional Apportionment*, p. 60.

[28] Representatives per million is computed by dividing the number of Representatives assigned to the state by the state's population (which gives the number of Representatives per person) and then multiplying the resulting dividend by 1,000,000.

[29] Montana argued in Federal court in 1991 and 1992 that the equal proportions formula violated the Constitution because it "does not achieve the greatest possible equality in number of individuals per Representative" *Department of Commerce* v. *Montana* 503 U.S. 442 (1992). Writing for a unanimous court, Justice Stevens however, noted that absolute and relative differences in district sizes are identical when considering deviations in district populations *within* states, but they are different when comparing district populations *among* states. Justice Stevens noted, however, "although common sense" supports a test requiring a "good faith effort to achieve precise mathematical equality *within* each State ... the constraints imposed by Article I, §2, itself make that goal illusory for the nation as a whole." He concluded "that Congress had ample power to enact the statutory procedure in 1941 and to apply the method of equal proportions after the 1990 census."

[30] The total area of the U.S. is 3,795,951 square miles. The area and (rank) among all states in area for the seven single district states in this scenario are as follows: Alaska–664,988 (1), Delaware–2,489 (49), Montana–147,039 (4), North Dakota–70,698 (19), South Dakota–77,116 (17), Vermont–9,616 (45), Wyoming–97,812 (10), Source: U.S. Department of Commerce, U.S. Census Bureau, *Statistical Abstract of the United States, 2010*, (Washington: GPO, 2010), Table 346: Land and Water Area of the States and Other Entities: 2008, p. 215.

[31] U.S. Census Bureau, Projections of the Total Population of States: 1995-2025, Series A, http://www.census.gov/ population/projections/stpjpop.txt. If the major fractions method

had been used to apportion the House in 2010, the number of states with a single Representative would have increased by one, from seven to eight, with the addition of Rhode Island.

The House of Representatives... ISBN: 978-1-61324-308-4
Editors: R. D. Orsino, O. G. Trance

Chapter 2

HOUSE APPORTIONMENT 2010: STATES GAINING, LOSING, AND ON THE MARGIN*

Royce Crocker

SUMMARY

On December 21, 2010, the Commerce Department released 2010 Census population figures and the resulting reapportionment of seats in the House of Representatives. The apportionment population of the 50 states in 2010 is 309,183,463, a figure 9.9% greater than in 2000. Just as in the 108th Congress, 12 seats will shift among 18 states in the 113th Congress as a result of the reapportionment. The next census data release will begin February 2011, when the Census Bureau will provide states the small-area data necessary to re-draw congressional and state legislative districts in time for the 2012 elections.

* This is an edited, reformatted and augmented version of a Congressional Research Services publication, dated January 13, 2011.

BACKGROUND

The Census Bureau's release of the first figures from the 2010 Census on December 21, 2010, will shift 12 seats among 18 states for the 113th Congress (beginning in January 2013). Illinois, Iowa, Louisiana, Massachusetts, Michigan, Missouri, New Jersey, and Pennsylvania will each lose one seat; New York and Ohio will each lose two seats. Arizona, Georgia, Nevada, South Carolina, Utah, and Washington will each gain one seat; Florida will gain two seats, and Texas will gain four seats.[1]

The reapportionment of House seats in 2010 is based on an apportionment population that is different from the actual resident population of each state. For apportionment purposes since 1970 (with the exception of 1980), the Census Bureau has added to each state's resident population the foreign-based, overseas military and federal employees and their dependents, who are from the state but not residing therein at the time of the census. In 2010, these additional persons increased the census count for the 50 states by 1,042,523, a little less than twice the number as in 2000. If the foreign-based military and federal employees had not been included in the counts, there would be no change in the apportionment of seats, although the order of seat assignment would change.

TABLES

Table 1 sets out the apportionment population as of April 1, 2000, and April 1, 2010; it also provides the resulting seat assignments of each of the 50 states. The table also illustrates the population change from 2000 (shown by total and percent), the current House seat allocation, and what it will be at the beginning of the 113th Congress, and the average sized congressional district for each state in the 113th Congress. For the 113th Congress, the national average size congressional district will be 710,767, and districts will range in size from 527,624 (for Rhode Island's two congressional districts) to a maximum of 994,416 (for Montana's single district).

Table 1. Apportionment of Seats in the House of Representatives Based on the 2010 Census

State	2000 Apportionment Population[a]	Seats in 108th Congress	2010 Apportionment Population[b]	2010 Overseas/ Federal[c]	Change from 2000 Total	Percentage Change from 2000	Seats in 113th Congress	Seat Change from 2000	2010 Average CD Population[d]
AL	4,461,130	7	4,802,982	23,246	341,852	7.66%	7		682,819
AK	628,933	1	721,523	11,292	92,590	14.72%	1		710,231
AZ	5,140,683	8	6,412,700	20,683	1,272,017	24.74%	9	1	710,224
AR	2,679,733	4	2,926,229	10,311	246,496	9.20%	4		728,980
CA	33,930,798	53	37,341,989	88,033	3,411,191	10.05%	53		702,905
CO	4,311,882	7	5,044,930	15,734	733,048	17.00%	7		718,457
CT	3,409,535	5	3,581,628	7,531	172,093	5.05%	5		714,819
DE	785,068	1	900,877	2,943	115,809	14.75%	1		897,934
FL	16,028,890	25	18,900,773	99,463	2,871,883	17.92%	27	2	696,345
GA	8,206,975	13	9,727,566	39,913	1,520,591	18.53%	14	1	691,975
HI	1,216,642	2	1,366,862	6,561	150,220	12.35%	2		680,151
ID	1,297,274	2	1,573,499	5,917	276,225	21.29%	2		783,791
IL	12,439,042	19	12,864,380	33,748	425,338	3.42%	18	-1	712,813
IN	6,090,782	9	6,501,582	17,780	410,800	6.74%	9		720,422
IA	2,931,923	5	3,053,787	7,432	121,864	4.16%	4	-1	761,589

Table 1. (Continued).

State	2000 Apportionment Population[a]	Seats in 108th Congress	2010 Apportionment Population[b]	2010 Overseas/ Federal[c]	Change from 2000 Total	Percentage Change from 2000	Seats in 113th Congress	Seat Change from 2000	2010 Average CD Population[d]
KS	2,693,824	4	2,863,813	10,695	169,989	6.31%	4		713,280
KY	4,049,431	6	4,350,606	11,239	301,175	7.44%	6		723,228
LA	4,480,271	7	4,553,962	20,590	73,691	1.64%	6	-1	755,562
ME	1,277,731	2	1,333,074	4,713	55,343	4.33%	2		664,181
MD	5,307,886	8	5,789,929	16,377	482,043	9.08%	8		721,694
MA	6,355,568	10	6,559,644	12,015	204,076	3.21%	9	-1	727,514
MI	9,955,829	15	9,911,626	27,986	-44,203	-0.44%	14	-1	705,974
MN	4,925,670	8	5,314,879	10,954	389,209	7.90%	8		662,991
MS	2,852,927	4	2,978,240	10,943	125,313	4.39%	4		741,824
MO	5,606,260	9	6,011,478	22,551	405,218	7.23%	8	-1	748,616
MT	905,316	1	994,416	5,001	89,100	9.84%	1		989,415
NB	1,715,369	3	1,831,825	5,484	116,456	6.79%	3		608,780
NV	2,002,032	3	2,709,432	8,881	707,400	35.33%	4	1	675,138
NH	1,238,415	2	1,321,445	4,975	83,030	6.70%	2		658,235
NJ	8,424,354	13	8,807,501	15,607	383,147	4.55%	12	-1	732,658
NM	1,823,821	3	2,067,273	8,094	243,452	13.35%	3		686,393

State	2000 Apportionment Population[a]	Seats in 108th Congress	2010 Apportionment Population[b]	2010 Overseas/ Federal[c]	Change from 2000 Total	Percentage Change from 2000	Seats in 113th Congress	Seat Change from 2000	2010 Average CD Population[d]
NY	19,004,973	29	19,421,055	42,953	416,082	2.19%	27	-2	717,707
NC	8,067,673	13	9,565,781	30,298	1,498,108	18.57%	13		733,499
ND	643,756	1	675,905	3,314	32,149	4.99%	1		672,591
OH	11,374,540	18	11,568,495	31,991	193,955	1.71%	16	-2	721,032
OK	3,458,819	5	3,764,882	13,531	306,063	8.85%	5		750,270
OR	3,428,543	5	3,848,606	17,532	420,063	12.25%	5		766,215
PA	12,300,670	19	12,734,905	32,526	434,235	3.53%	18	-1	705,688
RI	1,049,662	2	1,055,247	2,680	5,585	0.53%	2		526,284
SC	4,025,061	6	4,645,975	20,611	620,914	15.43%	7	1	660,766
SD	756,874	1	819,761	5,581	62,887	8.31%	1		814,180
TN	5,700,037	9	6,375,431	29,326	675,394	11.85%	9		705,123
TX	20,903,994	32	25,268,418	122,857	4,364,424	20.88%	36	4	698,488
UT	2,236,714	3	2,770,765	6,880	534,051	23.88%	4	1	690,971
VT	609,890	1	630,337	4,596	20,447	3.35%	1		625,741
VA	7,100,702	11	8,037,736	36,712	937,034	13.20%	11		727,366
WA	5,908,684	9	6,753,369	28,829	844,685	14.30%	10	1	672,454
WV	1,813,077	3	1,859,815	6,821	46,738	2.58%	3		617,665

Table 1. (Continued).

State	2000 Apportionment Population[a]	Seats in 108th Congress	2010 Apportionment Population[b]	2010 Overseas/ Federal[c]	Change from 2000 Total	Percentage Change from 2000	Seats in 113th Congress	Seat Change from 2000	2010 Average CD Population[d]
WI	5,371,210	8	5,698,230	11,244	327,020	6.09%	8		710,873
WY	495,304	1	568,300	4,674	72,996	14.74%	1		563,626
Total	281,424,177	435	309,183,463	1,039,648	27,759,286	9.86%	435	Nat. mean:	708,377
								Minimum:	526,284
House size: Const, Minimum [e]:			50					Median:	710,552
House size: Const, Maximum [e]:			10,306					Maximum:	989,415

Notes:

a See, "2000 Apportionment Results," table 1 at http://www.census.gov/population/apportionment/data/2000_apportionment_results.html./

b See, "A New Portrait of America, First 2010 Census Results," table 1 at http://2010.census.gov/news/press-kits/apportionment/apport.html.

c See, "A New Portrait of America, First 2010 Census Results," table 3 at http://2010.census.gov/news/press-kits/apportionment/apport.html.

d The average size congressional district for each state is calculated on the resident population for each state, which is the apportionment population minus the overseas military (and other federal) employees.

e Article 1, Section 2 of the Constitution establishes the minimum size of the House (one Representative per state), and a maximum (one for every 30,000 persons).

PRIORITY LISTS AND SEAT ASSIGNMENTS

The reapportionment process for the House relies on rounding principles, but the actual procedure involves computing a "priority list" of seat assignments for the states. The Constitution allocates the first 50 seats because each state must have at least one Representative. A priority list assigns the remaining 385 seats for a total of 435. **Table 2** displays the end of the "priority list" that will be used to allocate Representatives based on the 2010 Census apportionment population. The law only provides for 435 seats in the House, but the tables illustrate not only the last seats assigned by the apportionment formula (ending at 435), but the states that would just miss getting additional representation.[2]

Table 2. Population Needed to Gain or Lose a Seat Using the 2010 Census Apportionment Population

Seat	Last Seat Allocated	State	2010 Apportionment Population	Priority Value [a]	Pop. Needed to Gain or Lose Seat [b]
420	26	FL	18,900,773	741,349.31	-823,146
421	7	AL	4,802,982	741,116.21	-207,729
422	51	CA	37,341,989	739,481.57	-1,536,070
423	18	IL	12,864,380	735,407.66	-460,846
424	14	MI	9,911,626	734,698.60	-345,845
425	27	NY	19,421,055	733,000.49	-634,234
426	35	TX	25,268,418	732,494.84	-808,318
427	18	PA	12,734,905	728,006.06	-331,371
428	52	CA	37,341,989	725,121.34	-826,973
429	14	GA	9,727,566	721,055.17	-161,785
430	7	SC	4,645,975	716,889.51	-50,722
431	27	FL	18,900,773	713,363.71	-113,952
432	10	WA	6,753,369	711,867.60	-26,608
433	36	TX	25,268,418	711,857.03	-99,183
434	53	CA	37,341,989	711,308.24	-117,877
435	8	MN	5,314,879	710,230.58	-8,738
			Last seat assignment by law		
436	14	NC	9,565,781	709,062.86	15,753
437	9	MO	6,011,478	708,459.48	15,028
438	28	NY	19,421,055	706,336.94	107,057
439	13	NJ	8,807,501	705,164.44	63,276
440	2	MT	994,416	703,158.30	10,002
441	7	LA	4,553,962	702,691.59	48,858
442	6	OR	3,848,606	702,656.11	41,487
443	17	OH	11,568,495	701,443.04	144,928

Table 2. (Continued).

Seat	Last Seat Allocated	State	2010 Apportionment Population	Priority Value [a]	Pop. Needed to Gain or Lose Seat [b]
444	12	VA	8,037,736	699,595.12	122,192
445	54	CA	37,341,989	698,011.59	653,688
446	19	IL	12,864,380	695,626.00	270,086
447	37	TX	25,268,418	692,350.39	652,566
448	10	MA	6,559,644	691,447.19	178,195
449	19	PA	12,734,905	688,624.80	399,561
450	28	FL	18,900,773	687,414.47	627,339

Source: Computations of priority values and populations needed to gain or lose a seat by CRS. See CRS Report R41357, *The U.S. House of Representatives Apportionment Formula in Theory and Practice*, by Royce Crocker, for an explanation of formula for allocating House seats.

Notes:

a Each state's claim to representation in the House is based on a "priority value" determined by the following formula:

$PV = P / [n(n - 1)]^{1/2}$; where PV = the state's priority value, P = the state's population, and n = the state's n^{th} seat in the House. For example, the priority value of Oregon's 6th seat is:

$$PV_{OR6} = 3{,}848{,}606 / [6(6 - 1)]^{1/2}$$
$$= 3{,}848{,}606 / [30]^{1/2}$$
$$= 3{,}848{,}606 / 5.477225575$$
$$= 702{,}656.11$$

The actual seat assignments are made by ranking all of the states' priority values from highest to lowest until 435 seats are allocated.

b These figures represent the population a state would either need to lose in order to drop below the 435th seat cutoff, or to gain to rise above the cutoff. If, in the case of Oregon, 41,487 more persons had been counted in the Census, the state's priority value would have been increased to 710,230.56 which would have resulted in a new sequence number of 435 because Minnesota's ^{8th} seat would have occupied the 436th position in the priority list.

OPTIONS FOR STATES LOSING SEATS

The apportionment counts transmitted by the Census Bureau to the President (who then sends them to Congress) are considered final. Thus, most states that will lose seats in the 113th Congress have only one possible option for retaining them: urge Congress to increase the size of the House. Any other option such as changing the formula used in the computations, or changing the components of the apportionment population (such as omitting the foreign-based military and federal civilian employees) might only affect a small number of states if the House stays at 435 seats.[3]

As noted above, the 435-seat limit was imposed in 1929 by 46 *Stat.* 21, 26-27. Altering the size of the House would require a new law setting a different limit. Article 1, Section 2 of the Constitution establishes a minimum House size (one Representative for each state), and a maximum House size (one Representative for every 30,000, or 10,306 based on the 2010 Census). In 2013, a House size of 468 would be necessary to prevent states from losing seats they held from the 108th to the 112th Congresses, but, by retaining seats through an increase in the House size, other states would also have their delegations become larger. At a House size of 468, California's delegation size, for example, would be 56 instead of 53 seats.

THE REDISTRICTING PROCESS

The apportionment figures, released on December 21, 2010, are made up of three components: total resident population figures for the 50 states and the District of Columbia, the foreign-based military and other federal employees allocated to each state and DC, and the sum of these numbers, which become the apportionment population.

These numbers (minus DC) are all that is needed to reapportion the House, but most states need figures for very small geographic areas in order to draw new legislative and congressional districts.[4] The Census Bureau must provide small-area population totals to the legislature and governor of each state by one year after the census (e.g., April 1, 2011).

The Census Bureau data to be delivered by April 1, 2011 (some states will start receiving the information in February 2011), are often referred to as the P.L. 94-171 program data (89 Stat. 1023). This program provides to each state information from the 2010 Census. As such, the information is very limited—including age, race, and Hispanic origin. No other demographic information that might be useful to the persons constructing political jurisdictions, such as income or employment status, are available in the P.L. 94-171 data. Such data, however, are available from the results of the American Community Survey for geographic areas with populations as small as 20,000 persons.[5]

Census data are usually reported by political jurisdictions (states, cities, counties, and towns), and within political jurisdictions by special Census geography (such as Census designated places, tracts, block numbering areas, and blocks). The P.L. 94-171 program allows states, which participate in it (49 in 2010), to request Census data by certain nontraditional Census geography such as voting districts (precincts) and state legislative districts.[6] These special political jurisdiction counts enable the persons drawing the district lines to assess past voting behavior when redrawing congressional and state legislative districts.

In most states, redrawing congressional districts is the responsibility of the state legislature with the concurrence of the governor. In seven states, Arizona, California, Hawaii, Idaho, Montana, New Jersey, and Washington, a non-partisan or bi-partisan commission is responsible for drawing and approving the plans.[7] Some states have explicit deadlines in law to complete their congressional districting. Most do not, so the effective deadline for the legislatures or commissions to complete their work will be whatever deadlines are established in the states for filing for primaries for the 2012 elections.

Although many states have standards mandating equal populations, compactness, contiguousness, and other goals to not split counties, towns, and cities, federal law controls the redistricting process. Other than a requirement that multi-member states cannot elect Representatives at-large (2 U.S.C. 2c) however, no federal statutory law establishes explicit standards for redistricting. The principal laws that apply are the Supreme Court decisions mandating one person, one vote and the Voting Rights Act.

The fundamental federal rule governing redistricting congressional districts, *one person, one vote*, was promulgated by the Supreme Court in *Wesberry* v. *Sanders* (376 U.S. 7, 1964). The Court has refined that ruling in a series of cases culminating in *Karcher* v. *Daggett* (462 U.S. 725, 1983) that one person, one vote means that *any* population deviation among districts in a state must be justified, but the deviations from absolute equality may be permitted if the states strive to make districts more compact, respect municipal boundaries, preserve the cores of prior districts, or avoid contests between incumbents.[8]

Section 2 of the Voting Rights Act (VRA) applies nationwide. It prohibits states or localities from imposing a "voting qualification or prerequisite to voting or standard, practice or procedure ... in a manner which results in the denial or abridgement of the right to vote on account of race or color." Section 5 of the act applies only to certain jurisdictions, which must have their redistricting plans pre-cleared by a court or the Justice Department before they become effective.[9] The Supreme Court interpreted the VRA's application to redistricting in a series of cases responding, in part, to the extraordinarily complicated districts created by many states in the 1990s to maximize minority representation (beginning with *Shaw* v. *Reno*, 509 U.S. 630, 1993). The court ended the decade by establishing new principles concerning such practices: (1) race may be considered in districting to remedy past discrimination; (2) but, states must have a compelling state interest to ignore traditional redistricting principles and "gerrymander" to establish majority-minority districts; (3) courts will apply "strict scrutiny" to such assertions that racial "gerrymanders" are necessary to determine whether such plans are narrowly tailored to achieve the compelling state interest.

End Notes

[1] See Table 1 for each state's data. These allocations are based on a 435 seat House of Representatives. The 435-seat House was established in 1929 by the Permanent Apportionment Act, (46 Stat. 21, 26-27) which ended the 19th century practice of increasing the House size after every census but one. There have been no permanent increases in the House size for most of the 20th century.

[2] The figures in Table 2 for the "population needed to gain or lose a seat" are somewhat misleading because it is unlikely that one state's population total would be adjusted without others changing as well. Since the method of equal proportions used to allocate seats in the House uses all state populations simultaneously, changes in several state populations may also result in changes to the "populations needed to gain or lose a seat."

[3] After the 1990 Census Montana and Massachusetts challenged the apportionment formula, and the inclusion of the foreign-based military and civilians in the apportionment population. The Supreme Court affirmed the constitutionality of the equal proportions formula and the inclusion of the foreign-based military and civilians in the counts in two separate cases: *U.S. Dept. of Commerce v. Montana,* 112 S. Ct. 1415 (1992) and *Franklin v. Massachusetts,* 112 S. Ct. 2767 (1992).

[4] With respect to single-member states, this information would be used to draw state legislative and local political jurisdictions.

[5] For information about the 2005-2009 American Community Survey data, see http://www.census.gov/acs/www/ data_documentation/2009_release/. For information about the American Community Survey, see CRS Report R41532, *The American Community Survey: Development, Implementation, and Issues for Congress*, by Jennifer D. Williams.

[6] For a fuller discussion of this topic see the U.S. Census Bureau publication, *Strength in Numbers : Your Guide to Census 2010 Redistricting Data From the U.S. Census Bureau,* http://www.census.gov/rdo/.

[7] National Conference of State Legislatures, *Redistricting Law 2010*, pp. 143-145. California adopted a redistricting commission initiative in 2008 for state legislative districts, and extended it to U.S. congressional districts in a 2010 initiative vote.

[8] For a more thorough discussion of the legal issues, see CRS Report RS22479, *Congressional Redistricting: A Legal Analysis of the Supreme Court Ruling in League of United Latin American Citizens (LULAC) v. Perry,* by L. Paige Whitaker; CRS Report RS22628, *Congressional Redistricting: The Constitutionality of Creating an At-Large District*, by L.

Paige Whitaker; CRS Report RL30870, *Census 2000: Legal Issues re: Data for Reapportionment and Redistricting*, by Margaret Mikyung Lee and; CRS Report RS21593, *Redistricting and the Voting Rights Act: A Legal Analysis of Georgia v. Ashcroft*, by L. Paige Whitaker.

[9] Section 2: 42 U.S.C. Section 1973(a) (1996); Section 5: 42 U.S.C. Section 1973(c).

The House of Representatives... ISBN: 978-1-61324-308-4
Editors: R. D. Orsino, O. G. Trance

Chapter 3

APPORTIONMENT POPULATION AND NUMBER OF REPRESENTATIVES BY STATE: 2010 CENSUS*

United States Department of Commerce, United States Census Bureau

Table 1. Apportionment Population and Number of Representatives, by State: 2010 Census

State	Apportionment Population (April 1, 2010)	Number of Apportioned Representatives Based on 2010 Census	Change in Seats from Census 2000 Apportionment
Alabama	4,802,982	7	0
Alaska	721,523	1	0
Arizona	6,412,700	9	+1
Arkansas	2,926,229	4	0
California	37,341,989	53	0
Colorado	5,044,930	7	0
Connecticut	3,581,628	5	0
Delaware	900,877	1	0

* This is an edited, reformatted and augmented version of the United States Department of Commerce, United States Census Bureau's publication.

Table 1. (Continued).

State	Apportionment Population (April 1, 2010)	Number of Apportioned Representatives Based on 2010 Census	Change in Seats from Census 2000 Apportionment
Florida	18,900,773	27	+2
Georgia	9,727,566	14	+1
Hawaii	1,366,862	2	0
Idaho	1,573,499	2	0
Illinois	12,864,380	18	-1
Indiana	6,501,582	9	0
Iowa	3,053,787	4	-1
Kansas	2,863,813	4	0
Kentucky	4,350,606	6	0
Louisiana	4,553,962	6	-1
Maine	1,333,074	2	0
Maryland	5,789,929	8	0
Massachusetts	6,559,644	9	-1
Michigan	9,911,626	14	-1
Minnesota	5,314,879	8	0
Mississippi	2,978,240	4	0
Missouri	6,011,478	8	-1
Montana	994,416	1	0
Nebraska	1,831,825	3	0
Nevada	2,709,432	4	+1
New Hampshire	1,321,445	2	0
New Jersey	8,807,501	12	-1
New Mexico	2,067,273	3	0
New York	19,421,055	27	-2
North Carolina	9,565,781	13	0
North Dakota	675,905	1	0
Ohio	11,568,495	16	-2
Oklahoma	3,764,882	5	0
Oregon	3,848,606	5	0
Pennsylvania	12,734,905	18	-1
Rhode Island	1,055,247	2	0

State	Apportionment Population (April 1, 2010)	Number of Apportioned Representatives Based on 2010 Census	Change in Seats from Census 2000 Apportionment
South Carolina	4,645,975	7	+1
South Dakota	819,761	1	0
Tennessee	6,375,431	9	0
Texas	25,268,418	36	+4
Utah	2,770,765	4	+1
Vermont	630,337	1	0
Virginia	8,037,736	11	0
Washington	6,753,369	10	+1
West Virginia	1,859,815	3	0
Wisconsin	5,698,230	8	0
Wyoming	568,300	1	0
TOTAL[1]	309,183,463	435	

[1] Apportionment population includes the resident population for the 50 states, as ascertained by the Twenty-Third Decennial Census under Title 13, United States Code, and counts of overseas U.S. military and federal civilian employees (and their dependents living with them) allocated to their home state, as reported by the employing federal agencies. The apportionment population excludes the population of the District of Columbia.

The House of Representatives... ISBN: 978-1-61324-308-4
Editors: R. D. Orsino, O. G. Trance

Chapter 4

APPORTIONMENT OF THE U.S. HOUSE OF REPRESENTATIVES BASED ON THE 2010 CENSUS*

United States Department of Commerce

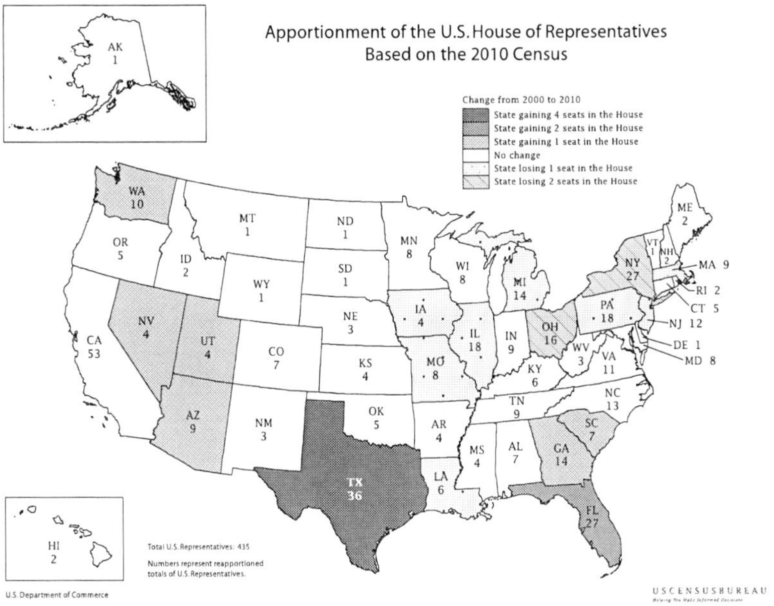

---

* This is an edited, reformatted and augmented version of the United States Department of Commerce's publication.

The House of Representatives... ISBN: 978-1-61324-308-4
Editors: R. D. Orsino, O. G. Trance

Chapter 5

OVERSEAS POPULATION OF THE 50 STATES AND THE DISTRICT OF COLUMBIA: 2010 CENSUS*

United States Department of Commerce, United States Census Bureau

Table 3. Overseas Population of the 50 States and the District of Columbia: 2010 Census

State	Overseas Population[1] (April 1, 2010)
Alabama	23,246
Alaska	11,292
Arizona	20,683
Arkansas	10,311
California	88,033
Colorado	15,734
Connecticut	7,531
Delaware	2,943
District of Columbia	2,875
Florida	99,463

* This is an edited, reformatted and augmented version of the United States Department of Commerce, United States Census Bureau's publication.

Table 3. (Continued).

State	Overseas Population[1] (April 1, 2010)
Georgia	39,913
Hawaii	6,561
Idaho	5,917
Illinois	33,748
Indiana	17,780
Iowa	7,432
Kansas	10,695
Kentucky	11,239
Louisiana	20,590
Maine	4,713
Maryland	16,377
Massachusetts	12,015
Michigan	27,986
Minnesota	10,954
Mississippi	10,943
Missouri	22,551
Montana	5,001
Nebraska	5,484
Nevada	8,881
New Hampshire	4,975
New Jersey	15,607
New Mexico	8,094
New York	42,953
North Carolina	30,298
North Dakota	3,314
Ohio	31,991
Oklahoma	13,531
Oregon	17,532
Pennsylvania	32,526
Rhode Island	2,680
South Carolina	20,611
South Dakota	5,581

State	Overseas Population[1] (April 1, 2010)
Tennessee	29,326
Texas	122,857
Utah	6,880
Vermont	4,596
Virginia	36,712
Washington	28,829
West Virginia	6,821
Wisconsin	11,244
Wyoming	4,674
TOTAL OVERSEAS POPULATION[1]	1,042,523

[1] Includes overseas U.S. military and federal civilian employees (and their dependents living with them) allocated to their home state or the District of Columbia, as reported by the employing federal agencies.

The House of Representatives... ISBN: 978-1-61324-308-4
Editors: R. D. Orsino, O. G. Trance

Chapter 6

CHANGE IN NUMBER OF STATES IN THE U.S. HOUSE OF REPRESENTATIVES, BY STATE, ORDERED BY SEATS GAINED AND LOST: 1940 TO 2010*

United States Department of Commerce, United States Census Bureau

Change in Number of Seats in the U.S. House of Representatives, by State, Ordered by Seats Gained and Lost: 1940 to 2010

State	Number of Seats in 1940	Number of Seats in 2010	Change
UNITED STATES	435	435	0
California	23	53	+30
Florida	6	27	+21
Texas	21	36	+15
Arizona	2	9	+7
Georgia	10	14	+4
Washington	6	10	+4
Colorado	4	7	+3

* This is an edited, reformatted and augmented version of the United States Department of Commerce, United States Census Bureau'spublication.

(Continued).

State	Number of Seats in 1940	Number of Seats in 2010	Change
Nevada	1	4	+3
Hawaii	*	2	+2
Maryland	6	8	+2
Utah	2	4	+2
Virginia	9	11	+2
Alaska	*	1	+1
New Mexico	2	3	+1
North Carolina	12	13	+1
Oregon	4	5	+1
South Carolina	6	7	+1
Delaware	1	1	0
Idaho	2	2	0
New Hampshire	2	2	0
Rhode Island	2	2	0
Vermont	1	1	0
Wyoming	1	1	0
Connecticut	6	5	-1
Maine	3	2	-1
Minnesota	9	8	-1
Montana	2	1	-1
Nebraska	4	3	-1
North Dakota	2	1	-1
South Dakota	2	1	-1
Tennessee	10	9	-1
Alabama	9	7	-2
Indiana	11	9	-2
Kansas	6	4	-2
Louisiana	8	6	-2
New Jersey	14	12	-2
Wisconsin	10	8	-2
Arkansas	7	4	-3
Kentucky	9	6	-3

State	Number of Seats in 1940	Number of Seats in 2010	Change
Michigan	17	14	-3
Mississippi	7	4	-3
Oklahoma	8	5	-3
West Virginia	6	3	-3
Iowa	8	4	-4
Massachusetts	14	9	-5
Missouri	13	8	-5
Ohio	23	16	-7
Illinois	26	18	-8
Pennsylvania	33	18	-15
New York	45	27	-18

* Not a state in 1940.

The House of Representatives... ISBN: 978-1-61324-308-4
Editors: R. D. Orsino, O. G. Trance

Chapter 7

CHANGE IN NUMBER OF SEATS IN THE U.S. HOUSE OF REPRESENTATIVES, BY REGION: 1940-2010*

United States Department of Commerce, United States Census Bureau

Change in Number of Seats in the U.S. House of Representatives, by Region: 1940 to 2010

	Seats in 1940		Seats in 2010		Numeric
Region	Number	Percent	Number	Percent	Change
UNITED STATES	435	100.00	435	100.00	-
Northeast	120	27.59	78	17.93	-42
Midwest	131	30.11	94	21.61	-37
South	135	31.03	161	37.01	+26
West	49	11.26	102	23.45	+53

- Represents zero.

* This is an edited, reformatted and augmented version of the United States Department of Commerce, United States Census Bureau'spublication.

The House of Representatives... ISBN: 978-1-61324-308-4
Editors: R. D. Orsino, O. G. Trance

Chapter 8

THE HOUSE OF REPRESENTATIVES APPORTIONMENT FORMULA: AN ANALYSIS OF PROPOSALS FOR CHANGE AND THEIR IMPACT ON STATES*

Royce Crocker

SUMMARY

In preparation for the reallocation of Representatives among the states based on the 2010 Census, it may prove helpful to examine the current House of Representatives apportionment formula. In addition, some members of the statistical community have, in the recent past, urged Congress to consider changing the current apportionment formula. Consequently, an examination of other methods that could be used to apportion the seats in the House of Representatives may contribute to a deeper understanding of the apportionment process.

Seats in the House of Representatives are allocated by a formula known as "the Hill," or equal proportions, method. If Congress decided to change it, there are at least five alternatives to consider. Four of these are based on rounding fractions and one, on ranking fractions. The current apportionment system (codified in 2 U.S.C. 2a) is one of the rounding methods.

---

* This is an edited, reformatted and augmented version of a Congressional Research Services publication, dated August 26, 2010.

The Hamilton-Vinton method is based on ranking fractions. First, the population of 50 states is divided by 435 (the House size) in order to find the national "ideal size" district. Next, this number is divided into each state's population. Each state is then awarded the whole number in its quotient (but at least one). If fewer than 435 seats have been assigned by this process, the fractional remainders of the 50 states are rank-ordered from largest to smallest, and seats are assigned in this manner until 435 are allocated.

The rounding methods, including the Hill method currently in use, allocate seats among the states differently, but operationally the methods only differ by where rounding occurs in seat assignments. Three of these methods—Adams, Webster, and Jefferson—have fixed rounding points. Two others—Dean and Hill—use varying rounding points that rise as the number of seats assigned to a state grows larger. The methods can be defined in the same way (after substituting the appropriate rounding principle in parentheses). The rounding point for Adams is (up for all fractions); for Dean (at the harmonic mean); for Hill (at the geometric mean); for Webster (at the arithmetic mean, which is 0.5 for successive numbers); and for Jefferson (down for all fractions). Substitute these phrases in the general definition below for the rounding methods:

Find a number so that when it is divided into each state's population and resulting quotients are rounded (substitute appropriate phrase), the total number of seats will sum to 435. (In all cases where a state would be entitled to less than one seat, it receives one anyway because of the constitutional requirement.)

Fundamental to choosing an apportionment method is a determination of fairness. Each apportionment method discussed in this report has a rational basis, and for each, there is at least one test according to which it is the most equitable. The question of how the concept of fairness can best be defined, in the context of evaluating an apportionment formula, remains open. Which of the mathematical tests discussed in this report best approximates the constitutional requirement that Representatives be apportioned among the states according to their respective numbers is, arguably, a matter of judgment, rather than an indisputable mathematical test.

INTRODUCTION

In preparation for the reallocation of Representatives among the states based on the 2010 Census, it may prove helpful to examine the current House of Representatives apportionment formula. In addition, some members of the statistical community have, in the recent past, urged Congress to consider changing the current apportionment formula.[2] Consequently, an examination of other methods that could be used to apportion the seats in the House of Representatives may contribute to a deeper understanding of the apportionment process.

In 1991, the reapportionment of the House of Representatives was nearly overturned because the current "equal proportions" formula[3] for the House apportionment was held to be unconstitutional by a three-judge panel of a federal district court. The court concluded that,

> By complacently relying, for over fifty years, on an apportionment method which does not even consider absolute population variances between districts, Congress has ignored the goal of equal representation for equal numbers of people. The court finds that unjustified and avoidable population differences between districts exist under the present apportionment, and ... [declares] section 2a of Title 2, United States Code unconstitutional and void.[4]

The three-judge panel's decision came almost on the 50th anniversary of the current formula's enactment.[5]

The government appealed the panel's decision to the Supreme Court, where Montana argued that the equal proportions formula violated the Constitution because it "does not achieve the greatest possible equality in number of individuals per Representative." This reasoning did not prevail, because, as Justice Stevens wrote in his opinion for a unanimous court, absolute and relative differences in district sizes are identical when considering deviations in district populations *within* states, but they are different when comparing district populations *among* states. Justice Stevens noted, however, that "although common sense" supports a test requiring a "good faith effort to achieve precise mathematical equality *within* each State ... the constraints imposed by Article I, §2, itself make that goal illusory for the nation as a whole." He concluded "that Congress had ample power to enact the statutory procedure in 1941 and to apply the method of equal proportions after the 1990 census."[6]

The year 1991 was a banner year for court challenges to the apportionment process. At the same time the Montana case was being argued, another case was being litigated by Massachusetts. The Bay State lost a seat to Washington because of the inclusion of 978,819 federal employees stationed overseas in the state populations used to determine reapportionment. The court ruled that Massachusetts could not challenge the President's decision to include the overseas federal employees in the apportionment counts, in part because the President is not subject to the terms of the Administrative Procedure Act.[7]

In 2001, the Census Bureau's decision to again include the overseas federal employees in the population used to reapportion the House produced a new challenge to the apportionment population. Utah argued that it lost a congressional seat to North Carolina because of the Bureau's decision to include overseas federal employees in the apportionment count, but not other citizens living abroad. Utah said that Mormon missionaries were absent from the state because they were on assignment: a status similar to federal employees stationed overseas. Thus, the state argued, the Census Bureau should have included the missionaries in Utah's apportionment count. The state further argued that, unlike other U.S. citizens living overseas, missionaries could be accurately reallocated to their home states because the Mormon church has excellent administrative records. Utah's complaint was dismissed by a three-judge federal court on April 17, 2001.[8]

The Supreme Court appears to have settled the issue about Congress's discretion to choose a method to apportion the House, and has granted broad discretion to the President in determining who should be included in the population used to allocate seats.

What, if any, challenges to the apportionment formula and process the country will face after the 2010 Census and apportionment remain to be seen. Although modern Congresses have rarely considered the issue of the formula used in the calculations, this report describes apportionment options from which Congress could choose and the criteria that each method satisfies.[9]

BACKGROUND

One of the fundamental issues before the framers at the constitutional convention in 1787 was the allocation of representation in Congress between the smaller and larger states. The solution ultimately adopted, known as the Great (or Connecticut) Compromise, resolved the controversy by creating a bicameral Congress with states represented equally in the Senate, but in proportion to population in the House.[10]

The Constitution provided the first apportionment: 65 Representatives were allocated to the states based on the framers' estimates of how seats might be apportioned following a census.[11] House apportionments thereafter were to be based on Article 1, section 2, as modified by clause 2 of the Fourteenth Amendment:

> Amendment XIV, section 2. Representatives shall be apportioned among the several States according to their respective numbers....
>
> Article 1, section 2. The number of Representatives shall not exceed one for every thirty Thousand, but each State shall have at least one Representative....

The constitutional mandate that Representatives would be apportioned according to population did not describe how Congress was to distribute fractional entitlements to Representatives. Clearly there would be fractions because districts could not cross state lines and the states' populations were unlikely to be evenly divisible. From its beginning in 1789, Congress was faced with questions about how to apportion the House of Representatives. The controversy continued until 1941, with the enactment of the Hill ("equal proportions") method. During congressional debates on apportionment, the major issues were how populous a congressional district ought to be (later recast as how large the House ought to be), and how fractional entitlements to Representatives should be treated. The matter of the permanent House size has received little attention since it was last increased to 435 after the 1910 Census.[12] The Montana legal challenge added a new perspective to the picture—determining which method comes closest to meeting the goal of "one person, one vote."

The "one person, one vote" concept was established through a series of Supreme Court decisions beginning in the 1960s. The court ruled in 1962 that state legislative districts must be approximately equal in population (Baker v. Carr, 369 U.S. 186). This ruling was extended to the U.S. House of Representatives in 1964 (Wesberry v. Sanders, 376 U.S. 1). Thus far, the "one person, one vote" concept has only been applied within states. States must be able to justify any deviations from absolute numerical equality for their congressional districts in order to comply with a 1983 Supreme Court decision—Karcher v. Daggett (462 U.S. 725).

The population distribution among states in the 2000 Census, combined with a House size of 435, and the requirement that districts not cross state lines, meant that there was a wide disparity in district sizes—from 495,304 (Wyoming) to 905,316 (Montana) after the 2000 Census. This *interstate* population disparity among districts in 2001 contrasts with the *intrastate* variation experienced in the redistrictings following the 1990 Census. Nineteen of the 43 states that had two or more districts in 1992 drew districts with a population difference between their districts of ten persons or fewer, and only six states varied by more than 1,000 persons.[13]

Given a fixed-size House and an increasing population, there will inevitably be population deviations in district sizes among states. What should be the goal of an apportionment method? Although Daniel Webster was a proponent of a particular formula (the major fractions method), he succinctly defined the apportionment problem during debate on an apportionment bill in 1832 (4 Stat. 516). Webster said that,

> The Constitution, therefore, must be understood, not as enjoining an absolute relative equality, because that would be demanding an impossibility, but as requiring of Congress to make the apportionment of Representatives among the several states according to their respective numbers, as near as may be. That which cannot be done perfectly must be done in a manner as near perfection as can be.[14]

Which apportionment method is the "manner as near perfection as can be"? Although there are potentially thousands of different ways in which the House could be apportioned, six methods are most often mentioned as possibilities. These are the methods of Hamilton-Vinton, "largest fractional remainders"; Adams, "smallest divisors"; Dean, "harmonic mean"; Hill, "equal proportions"; Webster, "major fractions"; and Jefferson, "largest divisors."[15]

Apportionment Methods Defined

Since 1941, seats in the House of Representatives have been apportioned according to the method of equal proportions (Hill)(see below, in "Rounding Methods").[16] However, from 1790 to the present, alternative methods for apportioning seats have been used or seriously considered. Six such methods stand out. One, the Hamilton-Vinton method, involves ranking fractional remainders. The others (the methods of Adams, Dean, Hill, Webster, and Jefferson) involve rounding fractional remainders.

Hamilton-Vinton: Ranking Fractional Remainders

Why is there a controversy? Why not apportion the House the intuitive way by dividing each state's population by the national "ideal size" district (645,632 in 2001) and give each state its "quota" (rounding up at fractional remainders of .5 and above, and down for remainders less than .5)? The problem with this proposal is that the House size would fluctuate around 435 seats. In some decades, the House might include 435 seats; in others, it might be either under or over the legal limit. In 2001, this method would have resulted in a 433-seat House (438 in 1991).

One solution to this problem of too few or too many seats would be to divide each state's population by the national "ideal" size district, but instead of rounding at the .5 point, allot each state initially the whole number of seats in its quota (except that states entitled to less than one seat would receive one regardless). Next, rank the fractional remainders of the quotas in order from largest to smallest. Finally, assign seats in rank order until 435 are allocated (see **Table 1**). If this system had been used in 2001, California would have one less Representative, and Utah would have one more.

This apportionment formula, which is associated with Alexander Hamilton, was used in Congress's first effort to enact an apportionment of the House. The bill was vetoed by President Washington—his first exercise of this power.[17] This procedure, which might be described as the largest fractional remainders method, was used by Congress from 1851 to 1901;[18] but it was never strictly followed because changes were made in the apportionments that were not consistent with the method.[19] It has generally been known as the Vinton method (for Representative Samuel Vinton (Ohio), its chief proponent after the 1850 Census). Assuming a fixed House size, the Hamilton-Vinton method can be described as follows:

> Hamilton-Vinton
>
> Divide the apportionment population[20] by the size of the House to obtain the "ideal congressional district size" to be used as a divisor. Divide each state's population by the ideal size district to obtain its quota. Award each state the whole number obtained in these quotas. (If a state receives less than one Representative, it automatically receives one because of the constitutional requirement.) If the number of Representatives assigned using the whole numbers is less than the House total, rank the fractional remainders of the states' quotas and award seats in rank order from highest to lowest until the House size is reached.[21]

The Hamilton-Vinton method has simplicity in its favor, but its downfall was the "Alabama paradox." Although the phenomenon had been observed previously, the "paradox" became an issue after the 1880 census when C. W. Seaton, chief clerk of the Census Office, wrote Congress on October 25, 1881, stating,

> While making these calculations I met with the so-called "Alabama" paradox where Alabama was allotted 8 Representatives out of a total of 299, receiving but 7 when the total became 300.[22]

Alabama's loss of its eighth seat when the House size was increased resulted from the vagaries of fractional remainders. With 299 seats, Alabama's quota was 7.646 seats. It was allocated eight seats based on this quota, but it was on the dividing point. When a House size of 300 was used, Alabama's quota increased to 7.671, but Illinois and Texas now had larger fractional remainders than Alabama. Accordingly, each received an additional seat in the allotment of fractional remainders, but since the House had increased in size by only one seat, Alabama lost the seat it had received in the allotment by fractional remainders for 299 seats.[23] This property of the Hamilton-Vinton method eventually led to a change in the formula in 1911.

One could argue that the "Alabama paradox" should not be an important consideration in apportionments, since the House size was fixed in size at 435, but the Hamilton-Vinton method is subject to other anomalies. Hamilton-Vinton is also subject to the "population paradox" and the "new states paradox."

The population paradox occurs when a state that grows at a greater percentage rate than another has to give up a seat to the slower growing state. The new states paradox works in much the same way—at the next apportionment after a new state enters the Union, any increase in House size caused by the additional seats for the new state may result in seat shifts among states that otherwise would not have happened. Finding a formula that avoided the paradoxes was a goal when Congress adopted a rounding, rather than a ranking, method when the apportionment law was changed in 1911.

Table 1 illustrates how a Hamilton-Vinton apportionment would be done by ranking the fractional remainders of the state's quotas in order from largest to smallest and compares it with simple rounding. In 2001, North Carolina and Utah's fractional remainders of less than 0.5 would have been rounded up by the Hamilton-Vinton method in order for the House to have totaled 435 Representatives.

Table 1. Apportioning the House in 2001 by Simple Rounding and Ranked Fractional Remainders (Hamilton-Vinton)

States Ranked by Fractional Remainders	Quota	Whole Number of Seats Assigned	Fractional Remainders	Hamilton-Vinton	Simple Rounding
North Dakota	0.995	1	0.99506	1	1
Virginia	10.976	10	0.97562	11	11
Maine	1.975	1	0.97500	2	2
Alaska	0.972	1	0.97215	1	1
Arizona	7.946	7	0.94600	8	8
Vermont	0.943	1	0.94271	1	1
Louisiana	6.925	6	0.92520	7	7
New Hampshire	1.914	1	0.91423	2	2
Alabama	6.896	6	0.89561	7	7
Hawaii	1.881	1	0.88058	2	2
Massachusetts	9.824	9	0.82386	10	10
New Mexico	2.819	2	0.81910	3	3
Tennessee	8.811	8	0.81060	9	9
West Virginia	2.802	2	0.80249	3	3
Florida	24.776	24	0.77601	25	25
Wyoming	0.766	1	0.76560	1	1
Georgia	12.686	12	0.68560	13	13
Missouri	8.666	8	0.66565	9	9
Colorado	6.665	6	0.66492	7	7
Nebraska	2.651	2	0.65146	3	3
Rhode Island	1.622	1	0.62247	2	2
Minnesota	7.614	7	0.61365	8	8
Ohio	17.582	17	0.58173	18	18
Iowa	4.532	4	0.53190	5	5
North Carolina	12.470	12	0.47028	13	12
Utah	3.457	3	0.45731	4	3
California	52.447	52	0.44715	52	52

Table 1. (Continued).

States Ranked by Fractional Remainders	Quota	Whole Number of Seats Assigned	Fractional Remainders	Hamilton-Vinton	Simple Rounding
Indiana	9.415	9	0.41458	9	9
Mississippi	4.410	4	0.40980	4	4
Montana	1.399	1	0.39936	1	1
Michigan	15.389	15	0.38882	15	15
New York	29.376	29	0.37617	29	29
Oklahoma	5.346	5	0.34633	5	5
Texas	32.312	32	0.31150	32	32
Wisconsin	8.302	8	0.30233	8	8
Oregon	5.300	5	0.29953	5	5
Connecticut	5.270	5	0.27015	5	5
Kentucky	6.259	6	0.25924	6	6
Illinois	19.227	19	0.22714	19	19
South Carolina	6.222	6	0.22157	6	6
Delaware	1.213	1	0.21349	1	1
Maryland	8.204	8	0.20445	8	8
South Dakota	1.170	1	0.16991	1	1
Kansas	4.164	4	0.16387	4	4
Arkansas	4.142	4	0.14209	4	4
Washington	9.133	9	0.13311	9	9
Nevada	3.095	3	0.09456	3	3
New Jersey	13.022	13	0.02160	13	13
Pennsylvania	19.013	19	0.01326	19	19
Idaho	2.005	2	0.00521	2	2
Total	435	413		435	433

Source: Data calculated by CRS. The "quota" is found by dividing the state population by the national "ideal size" district (645,632 based on the 2000 Census). North Carolina and Utah receive additional seats with the Hamilton-Vinton system even though their fractional remainders are less than .5.

Rounding Methods

The kinds of calculations required by the Hamilton-Vinton method are paralleled, in their essentials, in all the alternative methods that are most frequently discussed—but fractional remainders are rounded instead of ranked. First, the total apportionment population, (the population of the 50 states as found by the census) is divided by 435, or the size of the House. This calculation yields the national "ideal" district size. Second, the "ideal" district size is used as a common divisor for the population of each state, yielding what are called the states' quotas of Representatives. Because the quotas still contain fractional remainders, each method then obtains its final apportionment by rounding its allotments either up or down to the nearest whole number according to certain rules.

The operational difference between the methods lies in how each defines the rounding point for the fractional remainders in the allotments—that is, the point at which the fractions rounded down are separated from those rounded up. Each of the rounding methods defines its rounding point in terms of some mathematical quantity. Above this specified figure, all fractional remainders are automatically rounded up; those below, are rounded down.

For a given common divisor, therefore, each rounding method yields a set number of seats. If using national "ideal" district size as the common divisor results in 435 seats being allocated, no further adjustment of the divisor is necessary. But if too many or too few seats are apportioned, the common divisor must be varied until a value is found that yields the desired number of seats. (These methods will, as a result, generate allocations before rounding that differ from the states' quotas.) If too many seats are apportioned, a larger divisor is tried (the divisor slides up); if too few, a smaller divisor (it slides down). The divisor finally used is that which apportions a number of seats equal to the desired size of the House.[24]

The rounding methods most often mentioned (although there could be many more) are Webster ("major fractions"); Hill ("equal proportions"—the current method); Dean ("harmonic mean"); Adams ("smallest divisors"); and Jefferson ("greatest divisors"). Under any of these methods, the Census Bureau would construct a priority list of claims to representation in the House.[25] The key difference among these methods is in the rule by which the rounding point is set—that is, the rule that determines what fractional remainders result in a state being rounded up, rather than down.

In the Adams, Webster, and Jefferson methods, the rounding points used are the same for a state of any size. In the Dean and Hill methods, on the other hand, the rounding point varies with the number of seats assigned to the state; it rises as the state's population increases. With these two methods, in other words, smaller (less populous) states will have their apportionments rounded up to yield an extra seat for smaller fractional remainders than will larger states. This property, arguably, provides the intuitive basis for challenging the Dean and Hill methods as favoring small (less populous) states at the expense of the large (more populous) states.[26]

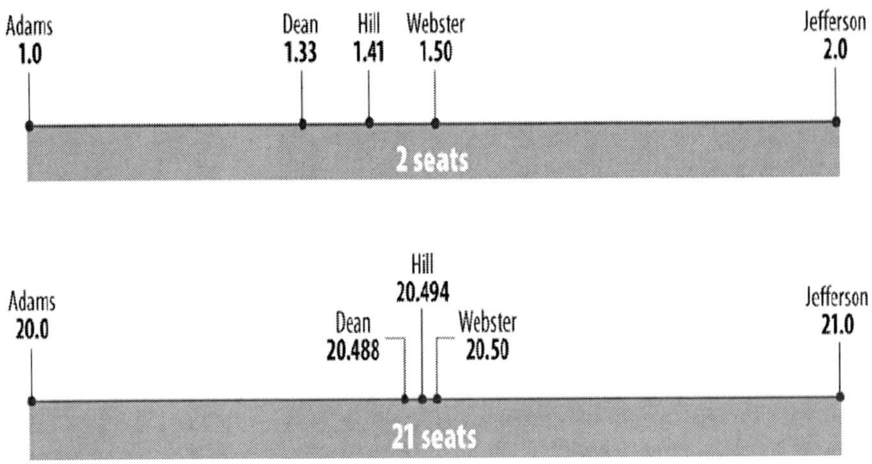

Source: This illustration is adapted from *Fair Representation*, pp. 63-65.

Figure 1. Illustrative Rounding Points for Five Apportionment Methods (For 2 and 21 Seats).

These differences among the rounding methods are illustrated in *Figure 1*. The "black dots" in *Figure 1* indicate the points that a state's fractional remainder must exceed for it to receive a second seat, and to receive a 21st seat. *Figure 1* visually illustrates that the only rounding points that change their relative positions are those for Dean and Hill. Using the rounding points for a second seat as the example, the Adams method awards a second seat for any fractional remainder above one. Dean awards the second seat for any fractional remainder above 1.33. Similarly, Hill gives a second seat for every fraction exceeding 1.41, Webster, 1.5, and Jefferson does not give a second seat until its integer value of a state's quotient equals or exceeds two.

Webster: Rounding at the Midpoint (.5)

The easiest rounding method to describe is the Webster ("major fractions") method which allocates seats by rounding up to the next seat when a state has a remainder of .5 and above. In other words, it rounds fractions to the lower or next higher whole number at the arithmetic mean, which is the midpoint between numbers. For example, between 1 and 2 the arithmetic mean is 1.5; between 2 and 3, the arithmetic mean is 2.5, etc. The Webster method (which was used in 1840, 1910, and 1930) can be defined in the following manner for a 435-seat House:

> Webster
>
> Find a number so that when it is divided into each state's population and resulting quotients are rounded at the arithmetic mean, the total number of seats will sum to 435. (In all cases where a state would be entitled to less than one seat, it receives one anyway because of the constitutional entitlement.)

Hill: Rounding at the Geometric Mean

The only operational difference between a Webster and a Hill apportionment (equal proportions—the method in use since 1941), is where the rounding occurs. Rather than rounding at the arithmetic mean between the next lower and the next higher whole number, Hill rounds at the geometric mean. The geometric mean is the square root of the multiplication of two numbers. The Hill rounding point between 1 and 2, for example, is 1.41 (the square root of 2), rather than 1.5. The rounding point between 20 and 21 is the square root of 420, or 20.494. The Hill method can be defined in the following manner for a 435-seat House:

> Hill
>
> Find a number so that when it is divided into each state's population and resulting quotients are rounded at the geometric mean, the total number of seats will sum to 435. (In all cases where a state would be entitled to less than one seat, it receives one anyway because of the constitutional entitlement.)

Dean: Rounding at the Harmonic Mean

The Dean method (advocated by Montana in 1991) rounds at a different point—the harmonic mean between consecutive numbers. The harmonic mean is obtained by multiplying the product of two numbers by 2, and then dividing that product by the sum of the two numbers.[27] The Dean rounding point between 1 and 2, for example, is 1.33, rather than 1.5. The rounding point between 20 and 21 is 20.488. The Dean method (which has never been used) can be defined in the following manner for a 435-seat House:

> Dean
>
> Find a number so that when it is divided into each state's population and resulting quotients are rounded at the harmonic mean, the total number of seats will sum to 435. (In all cases where a state would be entitled to less than one seat, it receives one anyway because of the constitutional entitlement.)

Adams: All Fractions Rounded up

The Adams method ("smallest divisors") rounds up to the next seat for any fractional remainder. The rounding point between 1 and 2, for example, would be any fraction exceeding 1 with similar rounding points for all other integers. The Adams method (which has never been used, but was also advocated by Montana) may be defined in the following manner for a 435-seat House:

> Adams
>
> Find a number so that when it is divided into each state's population and resulting quotients that include fractions are rounded up, the total number of seats will sum to 435. (In all cases where a state would be entitled to less than one seat, it receives one anyway because of the constitutional entitlement.)

Jefferson: All Fractions Rounded Down

The Jefferson method ("largest divisors") rounds down any fractional remainder. In order to receive 2 seats, for example, a state would need 2 in its quotient, but it would not get 3 seats until it had 3 in its quotient. The Jefferson method (used from 1790 to 1830) can be defined in the following manner for a 435-seat House:

Jefferson

Find a number so that when it is divided into each state's population and resulting quotients that include fractions are rounded down, the total number of seats will sum to 435. (In all cases where a state would be entitled to less than one seat, it receives one anyway because of the constitutional requirement.)

CHANGING THE FORMULA: THE IMPACT IN 2011

What would happen in 2011 if any of the alternative formulas discussed in this report were to be adopted? Using the 2000-2009 state population estimates provided by the U.S. Census Bureau,[28] a 2010 population distribution for the states may be projected using a linear estimating procedure.[29]

As compared to the Hill (equal proportions) apportionment currently mandated by law, the Dean method, advocated by Montana in 1991, would result (not surprisingly) in Montana regaining its second seat that it lost in 1991, and California not gaining a seat in 2011. The Webster method would cost Rhode Island a seat and give an additional seat to Texas relative to the current (Hill) method. The Hamilton-Vinton method would result in California not gaining a seat and Minnesota not losing a seat as compared to the current (Hill) method. The Adams method in 2010 would reassign 14 seats among 12 states (see Table 2) relative to the current (Hill) method. The Jefferson method would reassign 15 seats among 14 states (see Table 2) relative to the current (Hill) method.

Table 2 and Table 3, below, present seat allocations based on a projected 2010 Census population for the six methods discussed in this report. Table 2 is arranged in alphabetical order. Table 3 is arranged by total state population, rank-ordered from the most populous state (California) to the least (Wyoming). This second table facilitates evaluating apportionment methods by looking at their impact according to the population size of the states. Allocations that differ from the current method are *bolded and italicized,* as well as followed by an *asterisk* in both tables.

Table 2. Seat Assignments in 2010 for Various House Apportionment Formulas (Alphabetical Order)

State	Projected 2010 Apportionment Population	Quota[a]	Smallest Divisors (Adams)	Harmonic Mean (Dean)	Ranked Fractional Remainders (Hamilton-Vinton)	Current Method: Equal Proportions (Hill)	Major Fractions (Webster)	Largest Divisors (Jefferson)
Alabama	4,722,033	6.644	7	7	7	7	7	6*
Alaska	706,757	0.994	1	1	1	1	1	1
Arizona	6,816,325	9.591	10	10	10	10	10	10
Arkansas	2,911,097	4.096	4	4	4	4	4	4
California	37,255,448	52.423	50*	52*	52*	53	53	55*
Colorado	5,067,957	7.131	7	7	7	7	7	7
Connecticut	3,528,228	4.965	5	5	5	5	5	5
Delaware	897,619	1.263	2*	1	1	1	1	1
Florida	19,075,858	26.842	26*	27	27	27	27	28*
Georgia	10,038,872	14.126	14	14	14	14	14	14
Hawaii	1,308,549	1.841	2	2	2	2	2	1*
Idaho	1,577,524	2.220	3*	2	2	2	2	2
Illinois	12,937,086	18.204	18	18	18	18	18	19*
Indiana	6,454,439	9.082	9	9	9	9	9	9

State	Projected 2010 Apportionment Population	Quota[a]	Smallest Divisors (Adams)	Harmonic Mean (Dean)	Ranked Fractional Remainders (Hamilton-Vinton)	Current Method: Equal Proportions (Hill)	Major Fractions (Webster)	Largest Divisors (Jefferson)
Iowa	3,006,181	4.230	5*	4	4	4	4	4
Kansas	2,819,278	3.967	4	4	4	4	4	4
Kentucky	4,342,913	6.111	6	6	6	6	6	6
Louisiana	4,408,371	6.203	6	6	6	6	6	6
Maine	1,330,583	1.872	2	2	2	2	2	1*
Maryland	5,763,312	8.110	8	8	8	8	8	8
Massachusetts	6,578,643	9.257	9	9	9	9	9	9
Michigan	10,042,335	14.131	14	14	14	14	14	14
Minnesota	5,297,832	7.455	8*	7	8*	7	7	7
Mississippi	2,957,828	4.162	4	4	4	4	4	4
Missouri	6,034,391	8.491	9	9	9	9	9	8*
Montana	981,446	1.381	2*	2*	1	1	1	1
Nebraska	1,799,668	2.532	3	3	3	3	3	2*
Nevada	2,761,669	3.886	4	4	4	4	4	4
New Hampshire	1,343,413	1.890	2	2	2	2	2	1*

Table 2. (Continued).

State	Projected 2010 Apportionment Population	Quota[a]	Smallest Divisors (Adams)	Harmonic Mean (Dean)	Ranked Fractional Remainders (Hamilton-Vinton)	Current Method: Equal Proportions (Hill)	Major Fractions (Webster)	Largest Divisors (Jefferson)
New Jersey	8,734,543	12.291	12	12	12	12	12	12
New Mexico	2,029,960	2.856	3	3	3	3	3	3
New York	19,598,281	27.577	27*	28	28	28	28	29*
North Carolina	9,485,781	13.348	13	13	13	13	13	14*
North Dakota	641,905	0.903	1	1	1	1	1	1
Ohio	11,571,055	16.282	16	16	16	16	16	17*
Oklahoma	3,687,874	5.189	5	5	5	5	5	5
Oregon	3,859,470	5.431	6*	5	5	5	5	5
Pennsylvania	12,627,120	17.768	17*	18	18	18	18	18
Rhode Island	1,056,962	1.487	2	2	2	2	1*	1*
South Carolina	4,600,842	6.474	7	7	7	7	7	6*
South Dakota	815,863	1.148	2*	1	1	1	1	1
Tennessee	6,361,597	8.952	9	9	9	9	9	9
Texas	25,098,728	35.317	34*	35	35	35	36*	37*

State	Projected 2010 Apportionment Population	Quota[a]	Smallest Divisors (Adams)	Harmonic Mean (Dean)	Ranked Fractional Remainders (Hamilton-Vinton)	Current Method: Equal Proportions (Hill)	Major Fractions (Webster)	Largest Divisors (Jefferson)
Utah	2,835,918	3.990	4	4	4	4	4	4
Vermont	624,294	0.878	1	1	1	1	1	1
Virginia	7,980,639	11.230	11	11	11	11	11	11
Washington	6,715,594	9.450	9	9	9	9	9	9
West Virginia	1,816,881	2.557	3	3	3	3	3	2*
Wisconsin	5,693,015	8.011	8	8	8	8	8	8
Wyoming	540,885	0.761	1	1	1	1	1	1
TOTALS	309,142,868	435	435	435	435	435	435	435
Ideal CD Sizeb	710,673							

Source: Congressional Research Service.

Notes:

a A state's quota of Representatives is obtained by dividing the population of the state by the "Ideal Congressional District (CD) size."

b The "Ideal CD size" is obtained by dividing the total population of all the states (in this case, 309,142,868) by the size of the House of Representatives, 435.

Table 3. Seat Assignments in 2010 for Various House Apportionment Formulas (Ranked by State Population)

State	Projected 2010 Apportionment Population	Quota[a]	Smallest Divisors (Adams)	Harmonic Mean (Dean)	Ranked Fractional Remainders (Hamilton-Vinton)	Current Method: Equal Proportions (Hill)	Major Fractions (Webster)	Largest Divisors (Jefferson)
California	37,255,448	52.423	50*	52*	52*	53	53	55*
Texas	25,098,728	35.317	34*	35	35	35	36*	37*
New York	19,598,281	27.577	27*	28	28	28	28	29*
Florida	19,075,858	26.842	26*	27	27	27	27	28*
Illinois	12,937,086	18.204	18	18	18	18	18	19*
Pennsylvania	12,627,120	17.768	17*	18	18	18	18	18
Ohio	11,571,055	16.282	16	16	16	16	16	17*
Michigan	10,042,335	14.131	14	14	14	14	14	14
Georgia	10,038,872	14.126	14	14	14	14	14	14
North Carolina	9,485,781	13.348	13	13	13	13	13	14*
New Jersey	8,734,543	12.291	12	12	12	12	12	12
Virginia	7,980,639	11.230	11	11	11	11	11	11
Arizona	6,816,325	9.591	10	10	10	10	10	10
Washington	6,715,594	9.450	9	9	9	9	9	9

State	Projected 2010 Apportionment Population	Quota[a]	Smallest Divisors (Adams)	Harmonic Mean (Dean)	Ranked Fractional Remainders (Hamilton-Vinton)	Current Method: Equal Proportions (Hill)	Major Fractions (Webster)	Largest Divisors (Jefferson)
Massachusetts	6,578,643	9.257	9	9	9	9	9	9
Indiana	6,454,439	9.082	9	9	9	9	9	9
Tennessee	6,361,597	8.952	9	9	9	9	9	9
Missouri	6,034,391	8.491	9	9	9	9	9	8*
Maryland	5,763,312	8.110	8	8	8	8	8	8
Wisconsin	5,693,015	8.011	8	8	8	8	8	8
Minnesota	5,297,832	7.455	8*	7	8*	7	7	7
Colorado	5,067,957	7.131	7	7	7	7	7	7
Alabama	4,722,033	6.644	7	7	7	7	7	6*
South Carolina	4,600,842	6.474	7	7	7	7	7	6*
Louisiana	4,408,371	6.203	6	6	6	6	6	6
Kentucky	4,342,913	6.111	6	6	6	6	6	6
Oregon	3,859,470	5.431	6*	5	5	5	5	5
Oklahoma	3,687,874	5.189	5	5	5	5	5	5
Connecticut	3,528,228	4.965	5	5	5	5	5	5
Iowa	3,006,181	4.230	5*	4	4	4	4	4

Table 3. (Continued).

State	Projected 2010 Apportionment Population	Quota[a]	Smallest Divisors (Adams)	Harmonic Mean (Dean)	Ranked Fractional Remainders (Hamilton-Vinton)	Current Method: Equal Proportions (Hill)	Major Fractions (Webster)	Largest Divisors (Jefferson)
Mississippi	2,957,828	4.162	4	4	4	4	4	4
Arkansas	2,911,097	4.096	4	4	4	4	4	4
Utah	2,835,918	3.990	4	4	4	4	4	4
Kansas	2,819,278	3.967	4	4	4	4	4	4
Nevada	2,761,669	3.886	4	4	4	4	4	4
New Mexico	2,029,960	2.856	3	3	3	3	3	3
West Virginia	1,816,881	2.557	3	3	3	3	3	2*
Nebraska	1,799,668	2.532	3	3	3	3	3	2*
Idaho	1,577,524	2.220	3*	2	2	2	2	2
New Hampshire	1,343,413	1.890	2	2	2	2	2	1*
Maine	1,330,583	1.872	2	2	2	2	2	1*
Hawaii	1,308,549	1.841	2	2	2	2	2	1*
Rhode Island	1,056,962	1.487	2	2	2	2	1*	1*
Montana	981,446	1.381	2*	2*	1	1	1	1

State	Projected 2010 Apportionment Population	Quota[a]	Smallest Divisors (Adams)	Harmonic Mean (Dean)	Ranked Fractional Remainders (Hamilton-Vinton)	Current Method: Equal Proportions (Hill)	Major Fractions (Webster)	Largest Divisors (Jefferson)
Delaware	897,619	1.263	2*	1	1	1	1	1
South Dakota	815,863	1.148	2*	1	1	1	1	1
Alaska	706,757	0.994	1	1	1	1	1	1
North Dakota	641,905	0.903	1	1	1	1	1	1
Vermont	624,294	0.878	1	1	1	1	1	1
Wyoming	540,885	0.761	1	1	1	1	1	1
TOTALS	309,142,868	435	435	435	435	435	435	435
Ideal CD Size [b]	710,673							

Source: Congressional Research Service.

Notes:

a A state's quota of Representatives is obtained by dividing the population of the state by the "Ideal Congressional District (CD) size."

b The "Ideal CD size" is obtained by dividing the total population of all the states (in this case, 309,142,868) by the size of the House of Representatives, 435.

A Framework for Evaluating Apportionment Methods

All the apportionment methods described above arguably have properties that recommend them. Each is the best formula to satisfy certain mathematical measures of fairness, and the proponents of some of them argue that their favorite meets other goals as well. The major issue raised in the Montana case[30] was, which formula best approximates the "one person, one vote" principle? The apportionment concerns identified in the Massachusetts case[31] not only raised "one person, one vote" issues, but also suggested that the Hill method discriminates against more populous states.

It is not immediately apparent which of the methods described above is the "fairest" or "most equitable" in the sense of meeting the "one person, one vote" standard. As already noted, no apportionment formula can equalize districts precisely, given the constraints of (1) a fixed size House; (2) a minimum seat allocation of one; and (3) the requirement that districts not cross state lines. The practical question to be answered, therefore, is not how inequality can be eliminated, but how it can be minimized. This question too, however, has no clearly definitive answer, for there is no single established criterion by which to determine the equality or fairness of a method of apportionment.

In a report to Congress in 1929, the National Academy of Sciences (NAS) defined a series of possible criteria for comparing how well various apportionment formulas achieve equity among states.[32] This report predates the Supreme Court's enunciation of the "one person, one vote" principle by more than 30 years, but if Congress decided to reevaluate its 1941 choice to adopt the Hill method, it could use one of the NAS criteria of equity as a measure of how well an apportionment formula fulfills that principle.

Although the following are somewhat simplified restatements of the NAS criteria, they succinctly present the question before Congress if it chooses to take up this matter. Which of these measures best approximates the one person, one vote concept?

- The method that minimizes the difference between the largest average district size in the country and the smallest? This criterion leads to the Dean method.
- The method that minimizes the difference in each person's individual share of his or her Representative by subtracting the largest such share

for a state from the smallest share? This criterion leads to the Webster method.

- The method that minimizes the difference in average district sizes, or in individual shares of a Representative, when those differences are expressed as percentages? These criteria both lead to the Hill method.
- The method that minimizes the absolute representational surplus among states?[33] This criterion leads to the Adams method.
- The method that minimizes the absolute representational deficiency among states?[34] This criterion leads to the Jefferson method.

In the absence of further information, it is not apparent which criterion (if any) best encompasses the principle of "one person, one vote." Although the NAS report endorsed as its preferred method of apportionment the one currently in use—the Hill method—the report arguably does not make a clear-cut or conclusive case for one method of apportionment as fairest or most equitable.[35] Are there other factors that might provide additional guidance in making such an evaluation? The remaining sections of this report examine three additional possibilities put forward by statisticians: (1) mathematical tests different from those examined in the NAS report; (2) standards of fairness derived from the concept of states' representational "quotas"; and (3) the principles of the constitutional "great compromise" between large and small states that resulted in the establishment of a bicameral Congress.

Alternative Kinds of Tests

As the discussion of the NAS report showed, the NAS tested each of its criteria for evaluating apportionment methods by its effect on pairs of states. (The descriptions of the NAS tests above stated them in terms of the highest and lowest states for each measure, but, in fact, comparisons between all pairs of states were used.) These pair-wise tests, however, are not the only means by which different methods of apportionment can be tested against various criteria of fairness.

For example, it is indisputable that, as the state of Montana contended in 1992, the Dean method minimizes absolute differences in state average district populations in the pair-wise test. One of the federal government's counter arguments, however, was that the Dean method does not minimize such differences when all states are considered simultaneously. The federal government proposed variance as a means of testing apportionment formulas against various criteria of fairness.

The variance of a set of numbers is the sum of the squares of the deviations of the individual values from the mean or average.[36] This measure is a useful way of summarizing the degree to which individual values in a list vary from the average (mean) of all the values in the list. High variances indicate that the values vary greatly; low variances mean the values are similar. If all values in the lists are identical, the variance is zero. According to this test, in other words, the smaller the variance, the more equitable the method of apportionment.

If the variance for a Dean apportionment is compared to that of a Hill apportionment in 1990 (using the difference between district sizes as the criterion), the apportionment variance under Hill's method is smaller than that under Dean's (see *Table 4*). In fact, using average district size as the criterion and variance as the test, the variance under the Hill method is the smallest of any of the apportionment methods discussed in this report.

Table 4. Alternate Methods for Measuring Equality of District Sizes

	Criteria for Evaluation: Values to Be Minimized			
	Variance		Sum of Absolute Values of Differences	
Method	Average District Size	Individual Shares	Average District Size	Individual Shares
Adams	1,911,209,406	0.0354959	13,054,869	44.2368122
Dean	681,742,417	0.0077953	7,170,067	22.3962477
Hill (current)	**661,606,402**	0.0058026	7,016,021	21.3839214
Webster	665,606,402	0.0057587	6,997,789	21.2530467
Hamilton-Vinton	676,175,430	**0.0057013**	**6,977,798**	**21.0633312**
Jefferson	2,070,360,118	0.0112808	11,149,720	31.9326856

Source: Congressional Research Service.

Notes: ***Bolded*** and ***Italicized*** numbers are the smallest for the category. The closer the values are to zero, the closer the method comes to equalizing district sizes in the entire country.

Variances can be calculated, however, not only for differences in average district size, but for each of the criteria of fairness used in pair-wise tests in the 1929 NAS report. As with those pair-wise tests, different apportionment methods are evaluated as most equitable, depending on which measure the variance is calculated. For example, if the criterion used for comparison is the individual share of a Representative, the Hamilton-Vinton method proves most effective in minimizing inequality, as measured by variance (with Webster the best of the rounding methods).

The federal government in the Massachusetts case also presented another argument to challenge the basis for both the Montana and Massachusetts claims that the Hill method is unconstitutional. It contended that percent difference calculations are more fair than absolute differences, because absolute differences are not influenced by whether they are positive or negative in direction.[37]

Tests other than pair- wise comparisons and variance can also be applied. For example, *Table 4* reports data for each method using the sum of the absolute values (rather than the squares) of the differences between national averages and state figures.[38] Using this test for state differences from the national "ideal" both for district sizes and for shares of a Representative, the Hamilton-Vinton method again produces the smallest national totals. Of the rounding methods, again, the Webster method minimizes both these differences.

Fairness and Quota

These examples, in which different methods best satisfy differing tests of a variety of criteria for evaluation, serve to illustrate further the point made earlier, that no single method of apportionment need be unambiguously the most equitable by all measures. Each apportionment method discussed in this report has a rational basis, and for each, there is at least one test according to which it is the most equitable. The question of how the concept of fairness can best be defined, in the context of evaluating an apportionment formula, remains open.

Another approach to this question begins from the observation that, if representation were to be apportioned among the states truly according to population, the fractional remainders would be treated as fractions rather than rounded. Each state would be assigned its exact quota of seats, derived by dividing the national "ideal" size district into the state's apportionment population. There would be no "fractional Representatives," just fractional votes based on the states' quotas.

Quota Representation

The Congress could weight each Representative's vote to account for how much his or her constituents were either over or under represented in the House. In this way, the states' exact quotas would be represented, but each Representative's vote would count differently. (This might be an easier solution than trying to apportion seats so they crossed state lines, but it would, however, raise other problems relating to potential inequalities of influence among individual Representatives.[39])

If this "quota representation" defines absolute fairness, then the concept of the quota, rather than some statistical test, can be used as the basis of a simple concept for judging the relative fairness of apportionment methods: a method should never make a seat allocation that differs from a state's exact quota by more than one seat.[40] Unfortunately, this concept is complicated in its application by the constitutional requirement that each state must get one seat regardless of population size. Hence, some modification of the quota concept is needed to account for this requirement.

Fair Share

One solution is the concept of "fair share," which accounts for entitlements to less than one seat by eliminating them from the calculation of quota. After all, if the Constitution awards a seat for a fraction of less than one, then, by definition, that is the state's fair share of seats.

> To illustrate, consider a hypothetical country with four states having populations 580, 268, 102, and 50 (thousand) and a House of 10 seats to apportion. Then the quotas are 5.80, 2.68, 1.02 and .50. But if each state is entitled to at least one whole seat, then the fair share of the smallest state is 1 exactly. This leaves 9 seats to be divided among the rest. Their quotas of 9 seats are 5.49, 2.54, and .97. Now the last of these is entitled to 1 seat, so its fair share is 1 exactly, leaving 8 seats for the rest. Their quotas of 8 are 5.47 and 2.53. Since these are both greater than 1, they represent the exact fractional representation that these two states are entitled to; i.e. they are the *fair shares*.[41]

Having accounted for the definitional problem of the constitutional minimum of one seat, the revised measure is not the exact quota, but the states' fair shares. Which method meets the goal of not deviating by more than one seat from a state's fair share? No rounding method meets this test under all circumstances. Of the methods described in this report, only the Hamilton-Vinton method always stays within one seat of a state's fair share. Some rounding methods are better than others in this respect. Both the Adams and Jefferson methods nearly always produce examples of states that get more than one seat above or below their fair shares. Through experimentation we learn that the Dean method tends to violate this concept approximately one percent of the time, while Webster and Hill violate it much less than one percent of the time.[42]

Implementing the "Great Compromise"

The framers of the Constitution (as noted earlier) created a bicameral Congress in which representation for the states was equal in the Senate and apportioned by population in the House. In the House, the principal means of apportionment is by population, but each state is entitled to one Representative regardless of its population level. Given historians' understanding that the "great compromise" was struck, in part, in order to balance the interests of the smaller states with those of the larger ones, how well do the various methods of apportionment contribute to this end?

If it is posited that the combination of factors favoring the influence of small states encompassed in the great compromise (equal representation in the Senate, and a one seat minimum in the House) unduly advantages the small states, then compensatory influence could be provided to the large states in an apportionment formula. This approach would suggest the adoption of the Jefferson method because it significantly favors large states.[43]

If it is posited that the influence of the small states is overshadowed by the larger ones (perhaps because the dynamics of the electoral college focus the attention of presidential candidates on larger states, or the increasing number of one-Representative states—from five to seven since 1910), there are several methods that could reduce the perceived imbalance. The Adams method favors small states in the extreme, Dean much less so, and Hill to a small degree.[44]

If it is posited that an apportionment method should be neutral in its application to the states, two methods may meet this requirement. Both the Webster and Hamilton-Vinton methods are considered to have these properties.[45]

SUMMARY AND OVERVIEW

If Congress decides to revisit the matter of the apportionment formula, this report illustrates that there could be many alternative criteria from which it can choose as a basis for decision. Among the competing mathematical tests are the pair-wise measures proposed by the National Academy of Sciences in 1929. The federal government proposed the statistical test of variance as an appropriate means of computing a total for all the districts in the country in the 1992 litigation on this matter. The plaintiffs in Massachusetts argued that variance can be computed for different criteria than those proposed by the federal government—with different variance measures leading to different methods.

The contention that one method or another best implements the "great compromise" is open to much discussion. All of the competing points suggest that Congress would be faced with difficult choices if it decided to take this issue up prior to the 2010 Census. Which of the mathematical tests discussed in this report best approximates the constitutional requirement that Representatives be apportioned among the states according to their respective numbers is, arguably, a matter of judgment—rather than an indisputable mathematical test.

End Notes

[1] A similar, previous CRS report was authored by David C. Huckabee, who retired from CRS in 2005. While the current report is modified by the author, Mr. Huckabee's contributions, in large part, remain. Of course, any errors that may appear are due solely to the current author.

[2] See Brookings Institution Policy Brief, *Dividing the House: Why Congress Should Reinstate the Old Reapportionment Formula*, by H. Peyton Young, Policy Brief No. 88, (Washington, Brookings Institution, August 2001). Young suggests that Congress consider the matter "now—well in advance of the next census," p. 1

[3] CRS Report R41357, *The U.S. House of Representatives Apportionment Formula in Theory and Practice*, by Royce Crocker.

[4] *Montana v. Department of Commerce*, No. CV. 91-22-H-CCL (D. Mt. October 18, 1991). U.S. District Court for the District of Montana, Helena Division.

[5] 55 *Stat.* 761, codified in 2 U.S.C. 2a, was enacted November 15, 1941.

[6] Department of Commerce v. Montana 503 U.S. 442 (1992).

[7] *Franklin* v. *Massachusetts*, 505 U.S. 788 (1992). The Administrative Procedure Act (APA)(5 U.S.C, Subchaper II) sets forth the procedures by which federal agencies are accountable to the public and their actions are subject to review by the courts. Since the Supreme Court ruled that a President's decisions are not subject to review under the APA by courts, the

district court's decision to the contrary was reversed. Plaintiffs in this case also challenged the House apportionment formula, arguing that the Hill (equal proportions) method discriminated against larger states.

8 *Utah* v. *Evans*, No. F-2-01-CV-23: B (D. Utah, complaint filed January 10, 2000). Representative Gilman introduced H.R. 1745, the Full Equality for Americans Abroad Act, on May 8, 2001. The bill would require including all citizens living abroad in the state populations used for future apportionments. For further reading on this and other legal matters pertaining to the 2000 census, see CRS Report RL30870, *Census 2000: Legal Issues re: Data for Reapportionment and Redistricting*, by Margaret Mikyung Lee.

9 Representative Fithian (H.R. 1990) and Senator Lugar (S. 695) introduced bills in the 97th Congress to adopt the Hamilton-Vinton method of apportionment to be effective for the 1981 apportionment and subsequent apportionments. Hearings were held in the House, but no further action was taken.

10 For a discussion and analysis, see Charles A. Kromkowski, *Recreating the Republic* (Cambridge, UK: Cambridge University Press, 2002), pp. 261-307.

11 There was even a dispute over the first apportionment, see Kromkowski, pp. 287-294.

12 Article I, Section 3 defines both the maximum and minimum size of the House; the actual House size is set by law. There can be no fewer than one Representative per state, and no more than one for every 30,000 persons. Thus, the House after 2001 could have been as small as 50 and as large as 9,361 Representatives (30,000 divided into the total U.S. apportionment population).

13 CRS Archived Report 93-1060 GOV, *Congressional Redistricting: Federal Law Controls a State Process*, by Royce Crocker, pp. 53-54. This report is available to congressional staff from the author upon request.

14 M. L. Balinski and H. P. Young, *Fair Representation*, 2nd ed. (Washington: Brookings Institution Press, 2001), p. 31.

15 For a good survey of these methods, see Laurence F. Schmeckebier, *Congressional Apportionment* (Washington, D.C.: The Brookings Institution, 1941), pp. 12-58, and *Fair Representation*, pp. 10-35, 60-66.

16 For a thorough explication of the method of equal proportions, see CRS Report R41357, *The U.S. House of Representatives Apportionment Formula in Theory and Practice*, by Royce Crocker, esp. pp. 3-7.

17 *Fair Representation*, p. 21. Jefferson's method was used instead for all the apportionments from 1790-1831.

18 Schmeckebier, Congressional Apportionment. p. 73.

19 *Fair Representation*, p. 37.

20 The apportionment population is the population of the 50 states found by the Census.

21 Descriptions of each method of determining an apportionment in this report are blocked and *italicized* to set them off.

22 *Fair Representation*, p. 38.

23 *Ibid.*, p. 39.

24 Balinski and Young, in *Fair Representation*, refer to these as divisor methods because they use a common divisor. This report characterizes them as rounding methods, although they use common divisors, because the Hamilton-Vinton method also uses a common divisor, while its actual apportionment is not based on rounding. All these methods can be described in different ways, but looking at them based on how they treat quotients provides a consistent framework to understand them all.

[25] A "priority list" is a list of a state's "right" to the next House seat as determined by the rounding method used. For each seat (2 through 435), each state's "right" to its next seat is calculated. All of these calculations are ranked from highest to lowest and seats are assigned to each state based on the ranking in the "priority list." For a detailed explanation of how apportionments are done using priority lists, as well as how priority lists are constructed, see CRS Report R41357, *The U.S. House of Representatives Apportionment Formula in Theory and Practice*, by Royce Crocker.

[26] Peyton Young states that the Hill method "systematically favors the small states by 3-4 percent." He determined this figure by first eliminating from the calculations the very small states whose quotas equaled less than one half a Representative. He then computed the relative bias for the methods described in this report for all the censuses based on the "per capita representation in the large states as a group and in the small states as group. The percentage difference between the two is the method's relative bias toward small states in that year. To estimate their long-run behavior, I compute the average bias of each method up to that point in time." See, Brookings Institution Policy Brief No. 88, *Dividing the House: Why Congress Should Reinstate the Old Reapportionment Formula*, p. 4.

[27] Expressed as a formula, the harmonic mean (H) of the numbers (A) and (B) is: $H = 2*(A*B)/(A+B)$.

[28] U.S. Census Bureau, Population Division, "Annual Estimates of the Resident Population for the United States, Regions, States, and Puerto Rico: April 1, 2000 to July 1, 2009 (NST-EST2009-01)," (Washington: December, 2009), http://www.census.gov/popest/states NST-ann-est.html

[29] The estimating procedure used is taken from the 2003 MS Excel program functions—FORECAST.

[30] Department of Commerce v. Montana, 503 U.S. 441 (1992).

[31] *Franklin* v. *Massachusetts,* 505 U.S. 788 (1992).

[32] U.S. Congress, House, Committee on Post Office and Civil Service, Subcommittee on Census and Statistics, *The Decennial Population Census and Congressional Apportionment*, Appendix C: Report of National Academy of Sciences Committee on Apportionment, 91st Cong., 1st Sess., H. Rept. 91-1314 (Washington: GPO, 1970), pp. 19-21.

[33] The absolute representational surplus is calculated in the following way. Take the number of Representatives assigned to the state whose average district size is the smallest (the most over-represented state). From this number subtract the number of seats assigned to the state with the largest average district size (the most under-represented state). Multiply this remainder by the population of the most over-represented state divided by the population of the most under-represented state. This number is the absolute representational surplus of the state with the smallest average district size as compared to the state with the largest average district size. In equation form this may be stated as follows: $S=(a-b)*(A/B)$ where S is the absolute representation surplus, A is the population of the over-represented state, B is the population of the under-represented state, a is the number of representatives of the over-represented state, and b is the number of representatives of the under-represented state. For further information about this test, see Schmeckebier, *Congressional Apportionment*, pp. 45-46.

[34] The absolute representational deficiency is calculated in the following way. Take the number of Representatives assigned to the state whose average district size is the largest (the most under-represented state). From this number subtract the number of seats assigned to the state with the largest average district size (the most over-represented state) multiplied by the population of the under-represented state divided by the population of the over-represented

state. This number is the absolute representational deficiency of the state with the smallest average district size, as compared to the state with the largest average district size. In equation form, this may be stated as follows: $D=b-((a*B)/A)$ where D is the absolute representation deficiency, A is the population of the over-represented state, B is the population of the under-represented state, a is the number of representatives of the over-represented state, and b is the number of representatives of the under-represented state. For further information about this test, see Schmeckebier, *Congressional Apportionment*, pp. 52-54.

[35] To quote their rationale for selecting the method of equal proportions, After full consideration of the various methods, your committee is of the opinion that, on mathematical grounds, the method of equal proportions is the method to be preferred. Each of the other methods is, however, consistent with itself and unambiguous. The report goes on to state that, the best test of a desirable apportionment so far proposed is the following: If the "discrepancy" between A/a and B/b (Where A and B represent population and a and b represent number of Representatives) is defined to be the percentage of discrepancy:...This is accomplished only by using the method of equal proportions. Further, the report states, The method of equal proportions is preferred by the committee because it satisfies the test proposed above when applied either to sizes of congressional districts or to numbers of Representatives per person and because it occupies mathematically a neutral position with respect to emphasis on larger or smaller states. *The Decennial Population Census and Congressional Apportionment*, p. 21; The last statement of the NAS report was challenged by Balinski and Young in *Fair Representation,* pp. 55,76-78.

[36] In order to calculate variance for average district size, first find the ideal size district for the entire country and then subtract that number from each state's average size district. This may result in a positive or negative number. The square of this number eliminates any negative signs. To find the total variance for a state, multiply this number by the total seats assigned to the state. To find the variance for entire country, sum all the state variances.

[37] Declaration of Lawrence R. Ernst filed on behalf of the Government in Commonwealth *of Massachusetts, et al. v. Mosbacher, et al.* CV NO. 91-111234 (W.D. Mass. 1991), p. 13.

[38] This is not a "standard" statistical test such as computing the variance. This measure is calculated as follows. Each state's average size district is subtracted from the national "ideal size" district. (In some cases this will result in a negative number, but this calculation uses the "absolute value" of the numbers, which always is expressed as a positive number.) This absolute value for each state is multiplied by the number of seats the method assigns to the state. These state totals of differences from the national ideal size are then summed for the entire nation.

[39] For example, Virginia's quota of Representatives based on 2000 Census was 10.976. Based on this quota, each Virginia Representative would be entitled to 1.0976 votes each in the House. Their votes would "weigh" more than Alaska's single Representative whose vote would count 0.972 based on Alaska's quota.

[40] *Fair Representation*, p. 79.

[41] Balinski, M. L. and H. P. Young, *Evaluation of Apportionment Methods*, Prepared Under a Contract for the Congressional Research Service of the Library of Congress, Contract No. CRS 84-15, September 30, 1984, p. 3. Available to congressional staff from the author upon request.

[42] Ibid., p. 16.

[43] Table 3 rank-orders the states by their projected 2010 populations. The Jefferson method awards 55 seats to California and 37 seats to Texas when these states' quotas (state

population divided by 1/435 of the apportionment population) are 52.42 and 35.32 respectively.

[44] There is disagreement on this point as it pertains to the Hill method (*Declaration of Lawrence R. Ernst*) but the evidence that the Hill method is slightly biased toward small states is more persuasive than the criticism. See Balinski and Young, *Evaluation of Apportionment Methods*, noted above.

[45] *Evaluation of Apportionment Methods*, pp. 10-12.

The House of Representatives... ISBN: 978-1-61324-308-4
Editors: R. D. Orsino, O. G. Trance

Chapter 9

CONSTITUTIONALITY OF EXCLUDING ALIENS FROM THE CENSUS FOR APPORTIONMENT AND REDISTRICTING PURPOSES*

Margaret Mikyung Lee and Erika K. Lunder

SUMMARY

In the 2010 decennial census, the Census Bureau will attempt to count the total population of the United States. This includes, as in previous censuses, all U.S. citizens, lawfully present aliens, and unauthorized aliens. Some have suggested excluding aliens, particularly those who are in the country unlawfully, from the census count, in part so that they would not be included in the data used to apportion House seats among the states and determine voting districts within them.

One question raised by this idea is whether the exclusion of aliens could be done by amending the federal census statutes, or whether such action would require an amendment to the Constitution. The Constitution requires a decennial census to determine the "actual enumeration" of the "whole number of persons" in the United States. The data must be used to apportion the House seats among the states, although there is no constitutional requirement it be used to determine intrastate districts. It

---

* This is an edited, reformatted and augmented version of a Congressional Research Services publication, dated January 20, 2010.

appears the term "whole number of persons" is broad enough to include all individuals, regardless of citizenship status, and thus would appear to require the entire population be included in the apportionment calculation. As such, it appears a constitutional amendment would be necessary to exclude any individuals from the census count for the purpose of apportioning House seats.

From time to time, Congress has considered legislation that would exclude all aliens or only unauthorized aliens from being included in the census to apportion House seats among the states. Such legislation would have either amended the Census Clause of the Constitution or enacted or amended federal census statutes. In the 111th Congress, legislation has been introduced that uses both approaches. The Fairness in Representation Act would statutorily exclude aliens from the population count for apportionment purposes (H.R. 3797 and S. 1688). Under the above analysis, it would not appear to be constitutionally sufficient for Congress to amend the federal census statutes in such manner. Meanwhile, H.J.Res. 111 would take the other approach and amend the Constitution so that only U.S. citizens would be counted in the apportionment calculation.

Other legislation in the 111th Congress would not raise the same constitutional issues since they would not appear to require the exclusion of any individuals for apportionment purposes. An amendment introduced by Senator Vitter to the Commerce, Justice, Science, and Related Agencies Appropriations Act, 2010 (S.Amdt. 2635 to H.R. 2847), would have cut off funding for the census unless the census form included questions regarding citizenship and immigration status. The amendment was subsequently ruled to be non-germane. On the other side of the issue, the Every Person Counts Act (H.R. 3855) would prohibit the Census Bureau from asking about U.S. citizenship or immigration status.

INTRODUCTION

In the 2010 census, as in prior decennial censuses, the total population of the United States will be counted, including U.S. citizens, lawfully present aliens, and unauthorized aliens.[1] Some have asked whether aliens, particularly those in the country unlawfully, should be excluded from the census count.[2] It appears one concern is that these individuals are included in the data used to apportion House seats among the states and determine voting districts within them, which some perceive as unfair to states or districts with small alien populations.[3] One question raised by this idea is whether the exclusion of aliens could be done by amending the federal census statutes (Title 13 of the

U.S. Code), or whether such action would require an amendment to the Constitution.

The Constitution requires a decennial census to determine the "actual Enumeration" of the "whole number of persons" in the United States. [4] The data must be used to apportion the number of House seats among the states.[5] While not required by the Constitution, the data are used for other purposes as well, including by the states to determine voting districts within a state.

The Constitution expressly vests Congress with the authority to conduct the census "in such Manner as they shall by Law direct."[6] Congress has delegated this responsibility to the Secretary of Commerce and, within the Department of Commerce, to the Bureau of the Census.[7] The Census Bureau counts the total resident population of the states, with each individual counted at his or her "usual residence."[8] This includes both citizens and aliens.[9]

There is no legal requirement that the Census Bureau collect information regarding citizenship status. The 2010 census form sent to all households will not include questions regarding citizenship status or place of birth.[10] The Commerce Secretary has used his discretion[11] to ask for such information on the American Community Survey (ACS), which is sent monthly to a sampling of households.[12] Historically, questions regarding citizenship status have not been consistently included in the census population surveys.[13] At least two early censuses (1820 and 1830) included a category for foreigners not naturalized,[14] and later censuses asked about place of birth.[15] In modern times, the census questionnaire sent to all households has not included such questions, although the questionnaire sent to a sampling of households (the "long form," which has been replaced by the ACS) has asked for such information.

LEGISLATION IN THE 111TH CONGRESS

From time to time, Congress has considered legislation that would exclude all aliens or only unauthorized aliens from being included in the census to apportion House seats among the states. A discussion of selected legislation from prior Congresses is included in the *Appendix*. In the 111th Congress, several bills have been introduced that would amend the federal census statutes to explicitly address the treatment of unauthorized aliens. The Fairness in Representation Act (H.R. 3797 and S. 1688) would require the Commerce Secretary to include some means (e.g., a checkbox) for respondents to indicate they are U.S. citizens or lawfully present in the country on the census forms sent to all households. Additionally, the Commerce Secretary would be required to make adjustments to the data to prevent unauthorized aliens from being counted for apportioning House seats among the states.

An amendment introduced by Senator Vitter to the Commerce, Justice, Science, and Related Agencies Appropriations Act, 2010 (S.Amdt. 2635 to H.R. 2847) would have cut off funding for the census unless the census form included questions on U.S. citizenship and immigration status.[16] The amendment did not require the information be used for any purpose (i.e., to disregard certain individuals from the apportionment calculation). The amendment was subsequently ruled to be non-germane.

H.J.Res. 111 would amend the Constitution so that only U.S. citizens would be counted in the apportionment calculation. Specifically, it would amend the Constitution to read "Representatives shall be apportioned among the several States according to their respective numbers, which shall be determined by counting the number of persons in each State who are citizens of the United States."

On the other side of the issue, the Every Person Counts Act (H.R. 3855) would prohibit the Census Bureau from asking about U.S. citizenship or immigration status.

CONSTITUTIONAL ANALYSIS

While the Constitution permits Congress to conduct the census "in such Manner as they shall by Law direct,"[17] the census cannot be done in a way that is constitutionally impermissible. Thus, one question raised by the above legislation is whether they are consistent with the constitutional requirements for the decennial census.

It seems clear that Congress could, under its broad constitutional authority to conduct the census, statutorily require the Commerce Secretary to collect information regarding citizenship status.[18] The constitutionality of the other provisions in the legislation would appear to depend on whether all aliens are required to be included in the census count for any reason. If so, then it would appear that any exclusion would have to be done by constitutional amendment. On the other hand, if the Constitution requires such individuals to be excluded from the census count, then Congress could not prohibit the Commerce Secretary from asking questions about citizenship and immigration status.

As mentioned above, it appears some are concerned that aliens, particularly those individuals in the country unlawfully, are included in the data used to apportion House seats among the states and determine voting districts within the states. The next section analyzes whether Congress could statutorily exclude aliens from the census count for these purposes or whether any such exclusion would have to be done by constitutional amendment.

Data for Apportionment Purposes

Constitutional issues could arise if aliens were excluded by statute from the census count for purposes of apportioning House seats among the states. This is because it appears the term "persons" in the original Apportionment Clause and Fourteenth Amendment was intended to have a broad interpretation that is likely expansive enough to include unauthorized aliens. If true, any proposal to generally exclude unauthorized aliens would have to be in the form of a constitutional amendment.[19]

The term "persons/people" appears throughout the Constitution,[20] with its meaning evaluated in the context of each provision. On its face, the term's plain language meaning refers to individuals. However, it has been held to have a less obvious meaning in certain contexts; i.e., to include corporations for the Fourteenth Amendment's due process and equal protection guarantees.[21] Here, the question is whether the term refers to only a subset of individuals, U.S. citizens, for purposes of apportioning House seats among the states.

It seems that "persons" is not limited to "citizens" as the Framers would have likely used that term instead had it been their intent. The Constitution uses both the terms "persons/people" and "citizens of the United States," and the terms do not seem intended to be interpreted identically; rather, "citizens of the United States" appears to be a subset of "persons/people."[22] Courts have generally held that aliens, including unauthorized aliens, are "persons" in the context of other constitutional provisions, including other parts of the Fourteenth Amendment.[23] While it does not appear that any court has decided the meaning of the term "persons" for apportionment purposes,[24] a federal district court did state in dicta that the term clearly includes unauthorized aliens.[25]

It could be argued that certain aliens should not be included in the category of "persons" for purposes of apportionment because of their legal or voting status. On the other hand, historically, those without the right to vote or with inferior legal status, including women, children,[26] and convicts, have been included. It should also be noted that some states have historically permitted aliens to vote under certain circumstances.[27] Furthermore, the fact that slaves were to be partially counted when they enjoyed few rights seems to suggest the Apportionment Clause language was intended to be broadly inclusive.[28] Similarly, the fact that the Framers felt compelled to specify the exclusion of "Indians not taxed" may suggest "persons" was understood to otherwise include individuals residing within a state, regardless of legal status.[29] Thus, it can be argued that "[b]y making express provisions for Indians and slaves, the Framers demonstrated their awareness that without such provisions, the language chosen would be all-inclusive."[30]

The debates surrounding the original Apportionment Clause and the Fourteenth Amendment appear to add further support for the conclusion that the term "persons" was intended to be broadly interpreted. The Framers adopted without comment or debate the term "persons" in place of the phrase "free citizens and inhabitants" as the basis for the apportionment of the House,[31] thus suggesting the term "persons" includes free citizens and any other individuals who would be considered "inhabitants." According to James Madison, apportionment was to be "founded on the aggregate number of [the states'] inhabitants."[32] During the debate on the Fourteenth Amendment, Congress specifically considered whether the count was to be limited to persons, citizens, or voters.[33] The term "persons" was used instead of "citizens" due, in part, to concern that states with large alien populations would oppose the amendment since it would decrease their representation.[34] Another concern with using the term "citizen" was that it "would narrow the basis of taxation and cause considerable inequalities in this respect...."[35] Congress may also have been influenced by the fact that aliens could vote in some states.[36] Congress has subsequently considered excluding aliens from the apportionment calculation on several occasions,[37] and at least some Members have indicated that any such exclusion would have to be done through constitutional amendment since the Constitution otherwise requires total population as the basis for apportionment.[38]

Furthermore, while the Constitution expressly grants Congress the authority to grant citizenship,[39] it can be argued there is no indication that Congress was given similar power to grant the status of being a "person."[40] Thus, under this argument, Congress would not have the authority to statutorily exclude certain groups of individuals from the definition of "persons" and any such change would have to be done by amending the Constitution. On the other hand, it could be argued that Congress's broad constitutional authority over the census, apportionment, and immigration permits it to exclude certain aliens, particularly undocumented aliens.[41]

The argument could be made that counting aliens as "persons" for apportionment purposes dilutes the voting power of citizens in states without significant numbers of aliens and, therefore, is inconsistent with the Supreme Court's decision in *Wesberry v. Sanders*[42] that requires congressional districts be drawn equal in population to the extent practicable (i.e., "one person, one vote").[43] However, *Wesberry* and its progeny involve intrastate, as opposed to interstate, disparities,[44] and the Court has indicated in another line of cases that the *Wesberry* standard does not apply to interstate apportionment.[45] Because each state must have at least one House district and a fixed number of Representatives must be allocated among all states, votes in states with populations less than the ideal district are "more valuable than the national average" and it is "virtually impossible to have the same size district in any pair of States, let alone in all 50."[46] Therefore, while the goal of "complete equality for each voter" under the *Wesberry* standard is "realistic and appropriate for state districting decisions," the Court has explained that it is "illusory for the Nation as a whole."[47] While this second line of cases does not address the specific issue of whether aliens must be counted for apportionment purposes, the cases do seem to undermine the argument that *Wesberry* and its progeny require their exclusion.[48]

Some have pointed to the fact that the census has historically included questions about citizenship, thus perhaps suggesting that a distinction has been made between citizens and aliens for purposes of counting individuals. It is true that at least two early censuses (1820 and 1830) included a category for foreigners not naturalized[49] and later censuses asked about place of birth.[50] However, such information was not used to exclude any aliens from the census count. Rather, it is clear that such individuals were included in the total count,[51] and it appears the data was collected for informational purposes (similar to how information was collected about age, occupation, etc). It does not appear that aliens have been excluded from any census.

Data Used for Intrastate Redistricting

The U.S. Constitution does not require the use of federal decennial census data for intrastate congressional and state legislative redistricting. It only provides for the use of census data for apportionment among the states, not for redistricting and reapportionment within them. Federal courts have held that states are not required to use federal census data for redistricting, and therefore states can determine what data will be used for redistricting within a state.[52]

Federal courts have considered cases where state legislatures did not use federal decennial census data or even total population data as the basis for redistricting activities. Depending on the factual circumstances, the courts have upheld or invalidated the use of alternatives to official federal decennial data or total population data. For example, in the 1969 decision *Kirkpatrick v. Preisler*[53] involving Missouri's congressional redistricting plan, the Supreme Court, while invalidating the plan, nevertheless indicated that the use of projected population figures was not *per se* unconstitutional and that states may properly consider such statistical data if such data would have a high degree of accuracy (however, the Court also stated that the federal decennial census data were the best data available). In *Kirkpatrick*, the state legislature apparently performed rather haphazard adjustments and projections based on total population and the Court found that the legislature had not justified its methodology. In *Burns v. Richardson*,[54] the Supreme Court held that, in state legislative redistricting cases, the Constitution "does not require the states to use total population figures derived from the federal census as the standard" of measurement. The Court noted that in earlier cases it was careful to leave open the question of what population basis was appropriate in redistricting activities, even though in several cases total population figures were in fact the basis for comparison when determining whether the Equal Protection Clause of the Constitution had been violated. The Court recognized that, in a particular case, total population might not be the appropriate basis for redistricting plans. In the *Burns* case, Hawaii had used the number of registered voters as the basis for redistricting the state senate. The Court found that the redistricting plan "satisfies the Equal Protection Clause only because on this record it was found to have produced a distribution of legislators not substantially different from that which would have resulted from the use of a permissible population basis."[55] Hawaii was found to have a unique situation, wherein the significant number of tourists, military personnel, and other transient population segments distorted the distribution of actual state citizens. The redistricting plan that would have resulted from a total population basis would not have reflected the true state population distribution as accurately as a state citizen population basis. Since a registered voter population basis was the closest approximation of a state citizen population basis, the use of the registered voter population basis was deemed consistent with the Equal Protection Clause. However, the Court was careful to note that the ruling in the *Burns* case did not establish the validity of the unique redistricting population basis for all times or circumstances.[56] Although the federal decennial census figures need not be used as the basis for state redistricting, any alternate figures used must be shown to be the best data available or to be justified by particular circumstances as resulting in a more accurate redistricting plan than one based on federal decennial census total population figures.

The U.S. Supreme Court has not ruled on the constitutionality or propriety of using total population versus voting population as the basis for intrastate redistricting in a circumstance where the use of total population results in a disparity in voter strength in one district over another, although there is total population equality between the districts. In *Garza v. County of Los Angeles*,[57] the U.S. Court of Appeals for the Ninth Circuit held that redistricting based on voting populations instead of the total population would have been unconstitutional. Total population had been used as the basis of a court-ordered redistricting plan that was disputed by the County of Los Angeles. Justice Thomas, in his dissent from a denial of a writ of certiorari in *Chen v. City of Houston,*[58] contrasts the decision of the Ninth Circuit in *Garza* with those in which the U.S. Courts of Appeals for the Fourth and Fifth Circuits have held that the decision about whether to use total population versus voting population as the basis for redistricting within a state is a choice left to the legislative and political process.[59]

Since, under the Federal Constitution, the states arguably can and should use data other than the official apportionment census data in their own redistricting process if they know the other data to be the best available data, one must look at each state's laws to determine whether the states themselves require the use of official federal decennial census data in the redistricting processes. Although it appears that generally states prescribe a redistricting procedure by statute for state legislative redistricting, many do not have a statutory procedure for congressional redistricting. The state legislatures in such states conduct the congressional redistricting on an *ad hoc* basis after a federal decennial census. This means that in such states there may be no explicit statutory requirement to use official federal decennial census data for congressional redistricting, although there may be such an explicit requirement for state legislative redistricting. To the extent that a state's own laws do not explicitly require the use of official federal decennial census data for intrastate redistricting, the state is free to use any other data.

It might be suggested that the federal government release two official sets of data, one for apportionment of the House of Representatives among the states and the other for other purposes. In such a situation, it could be unclear what a reference in state law to official federal decennial census data would mean. Arguably, the second data set could still be considered official federal decennial census data , even though not used for apportionment purposes.[60] However, it should be noted that the Court's holding on standing for the plaintiffs in *Department of Commerce v. U.S. House of Representatives* indicates that a majority of the Court considers the references to official federal decennial census data to be a reference to the apportionment data.[61]

At the time of the decision in *Department of Commerce v. U.S. House of Representatives*, there was a flurry of state legislative activity concerning the type of federal decennial census data to be used in intrastate redistricting because of the absence of sufficiently clear and explicit statutory guidelines concerning the appropriate data to be used in intrastate congressional and state legislative redistricting activities.[62] Although there apparently has been no recent congressional activity concerning state redistricting census data, there is a potential role for Congress in determining what data will likely be used by the states.

Although Congress has not explicitly required states to use federal decennial census data in congressional redistricting, it could arguably do so under the same constitutional powers which give Congress the authority to establish other redistricting guidelines if it chooses, Art. I, § 2, cl. 1, which provides that the Members of the House of Representatives shall be chosen by the People and Art. I, § 4, cl. 1, giving Congress the authority to determine the times, places and manner of holding elections for Members of Congress. Where it is not clear that one data set is more accurate than the other and the constitutional goal of equal representation is not implicated, arguably, Congress could require that a particular type of data, including citizens only or including aliens, must be used in congressional redistricting. However, it could not do so with regard to the redrawing of state legislative or municipal districts, which remain the prerogative of the states as long as no constitutional voting rights are violated.

CONCLUSION

The Constitution requires a decennial census to determine the "actual enumeration" of the "whole number of persons" in the United States. The data must be used to apportion the House seats among the states, although there is no constitutional requirement it be used to determine voting districts within the states. The term "whole number of persons" appears broad enough to include all individuals, regardless of citizenship status, and thus would appear to require the entire population be included in the apportionment calculation. As such, a constitutional amendment, such as that found in H.J.Res. 111, would likely be necessary in order to exclude any individuals from the census count for the purpose of apportioning House seats. Legislation such as the Fairness in Representation Act (H.R. 3797 and S. 1688), which would amend the federal census statutes to exclude aliens from the population count for apportionment purposes, would therefore seem to be constitutionally insufficient.

APPENDIX. SELECTED LEGISLATION TO EXCLUDE ALIENS FROM THE CENSUS

From time to time, Congress has considered legislation that would exclude all aliens or only unauthorized aliens from being included in the census to apportion the House seats among the states. Such legislation would have either amended the Census Clause of the Constitution or enacted or amended federal census statutes.[63] Generally, the legislation providing only for statutory exclusions of aliens from the census failed because members recognized the potential unconstitutionality of these statutory restrictions. However, Congress has also consistently not adopted resolutions to amend the Constitution to exclude aliens, with members citing various reasons, including the reversal of constitutional tradition.

Some proponents of excluding aliens from the apportionment census have asserted that the framers of the Constitution did not understand the term "persons" necessarily to include aliens and point to the first census statute in 1790, which refers to "inhabitants," to support this contention. Since some of the members of the first Congress had been members of the Constitutional Convention a few years earlier, proponents argue that they must have known the intent of the Constitutional Convention in the Census Clause and would not have enacted an unconstitutional census statute. The proponents further argue that the term "inhabitants" in the first census statute was understood to refer to U.S. citizens only and not to foreigners/aliens, citing contemporaneous dictionary definitions. However, there is no direct evidence that this was the intention and, in fact, the early censuses apparently included aliens.

The 1790, 1800, and 1810 censuses included categories for free white males, free white females, other free persons, and slaves.[64] Free white persons were categorized further by age. The 1820 census was the first to include a subcategory for "foreigners not naturalized." Instructions to the federal marshals conducting the 1820 census noted that the data for this subcategory was not supposed to be added to the total data for free persons subcategorized by race and age, because they were already included as free persons.[65] These instructions appear to imply that the earlier censuses included free foreigners as well as free citizens in the data for free persons and that the new subcategory of information was not adding persons who would not have been counted under existing subcategories in earlier censuses.

In 1866, Congress considered constitutional amendments that would have limited the apportionment and census to voters or citizens. Such amendments were considered in the context of the civil rights amendments (ultimately resulting in the Thirteenth, Fourteenth and Fifteenth Amendments) being debated after the Civil War. The Fourteenth Amendment revised the apportionment clause, deleting the phrase counting three-fifths of slaves and instead requiring that the whole number of persons in each state must be counted, excluding Indians not taxed. However, if male inhabitants who were 21 years old and U.S. citizens were disenfranchised by a state for reasons other than participation in the Confederate rebellion or a crime, the population count of that state for purposes of apportionment would be reduced by the ratio of these disenfranchised male citizens to the total number of male citizens in that state. This was intended to discourage former slave states from disenfranchising former slaves and other African-Americans. A similar proposal would have counted the "whole number of persons except those to whom civil or political rights or privileges are denied or abridged by the constitution or laws of any State on account of race or color."[66] Some versions of this type of proposal would not have excluded Indians not taxed, while others kept the language excluding Indians not taxed.

During consideration of the civil rights amendments, an alternate type of proposal to amend the constitutional requirements for apportionment and the census would have counted only voters in each state to discourage former slave states from disenfranchising former slaves and other African-Americans.[67] However, this proposal was deemed flawed because it would also penalize other states by not including aliens/non-citizens in the census count for apportionment, since generally aliens were not permitted to vote in most states. Opponents also noted that this proposal would depart radically from the counting of all persons required by the original census clause. Another criticism was that suffrage would be cheapened because states would reduce or eliminate legitimate conditions for voter eligibility in an attempt to increase the number of voters. Some proposals to count voters or electors would have excluded citizens who had been disenfranchised as former

Confederate rebels, while others would have included such citizens. Some voter-based apportionment census proposals were brought up for floor votes and failed.

For proponents, the type of proposals that evolved into the Fourteenth Amendment had the advantage of not penalizing states that were not former slave states, but had high numbers of aliens. Meanwhile, this type of legislation would still effectively discourage former slave states from disenfranchising former slaves, since such disenfranchised persons would not be counted at all, a significant reduction from being counted at a three-fifths ratio.

In the late 1920s and early 1930s, the issue of counting aliens was raised as Congress considered legislation for the 1930 census and related apportionment of the House of Representatives. Apportionment was such a contentious issue following the 1920 census that the requisite decennial apportionment of the House of Representatives was never completed. The apportionment had been directly legislated by Congress until the 1920 census. After the breakdown in the process, Congress legislated a formula for calculating and allocating the Representatives among the states, thus eliminating the partisan negotiations that had hampered earlier apportionments and impeded/prevented apportionment in the 1920s. As Congress considered the appropriate apportionment formula, it debated whether to amend the Constitution to exclude aliens from the census data used for the apportionment. A 1929 Senate Legislative Counsel opinion analyzing such proposals, concluded that "there is no constitutional authority for the enactment of legislation excluding aliens from enumeration for purposes of apportionment of Representatives among the States."[68] While acknowledging that no case law had ruled on the issue of the meaning of "persons" in the Census Clause, the opinion found that according to rules of statutory construction, "persons" had at all times been understood to include aliens. Additionally, the reference in the Fourteenth Amendment to excluding Indians not taxed would be unnecessary if "persons" referred only to citizens and the Fourteenth Amendment would not have explicitly referred later in the same clause to the number of male inhabitants who were citizens and 21 years old. With regard to the original apportionment and census language, the opinion contrasted the use of the word "person" with the use of the word "citizen" for particular reasons in other parts of the original Constitution. Proposals to exclude aliens by statute alone failed as unconstitutional. Proposals to amend the constitutional language also failed.[69]

In 1940, when asked by a colleague whether the census for apportionment must count aliens unlawfully present in the United States, Representative Celler asserted that a constitutional amendment would be required to exclude even unlawfully present aliens from the census.[70] Earlier congressional debates apparently do not discuss unauthorized aliens, but rather consider the constitutionality and/or policy of excluding lawful aliens.

In the late 1970s and the 1980s, Congress considered immigration legislation that became the Immigration Reform and Control Act of 1986, which legalized certain unauthorized aliens and strengthened immigration laws to prevent immigration fraud, provide greater protections for temporary foreign workers and prevent displacement of U.S. workers, etc. In the period before and after the enactment of this legislation, Congress also considered proposals to exclude aliens from the census, including proposals specifically to exclude unauthorized aliens.[71] The latter proposals appear to be related to the proposals to legalize or strengthen enforcement against unauthorized aliens. Some members noted that unauthorized aliens needed to be included in the census in order to assess the potential impact of legalization.

A key legislative proposal in the late 1980s resembled the Vitter amendment in the 111th Congress to prohibit the use of funds to include illegal aliens in the census for apportionment of the House of Representatives. This provision was sponsored by Senator Shelby as amendments to the bill for appropriations to the Departments of Commerce, Justice, and State (CJS appropriations bill)[72] and the Senate-passed version of the Immigration Act of 1990.[73] Although such provisions were passed by the Senate in these bills, they ultimately were not enacted. House proponents of this proposal failed in their attempt to have the House instruct its conferees for the CJS appropriations bill to retain the Senate provision in their negotiations;[74] there had been no such provision in the House-passed version. The House conferees objected to the provision and it was dropped. However, the House floor debate on instructions to the conferees was echoed by the debates in the 111th Congress.

End Notes

[1] The three main components of the unauthorized resident alien population are (1) aliens who overstay their nonimmigrant visas, (2) aliens who enter the country surreptitiously without inspection, and (3) aliens who are admitted on the basis of fraudulent documents.

[2] *See, e.g.*, John S. Baker and Elliott Stonecipher, *Our Unconstitutional Census*, WALL ST. J., Aug. 9, 2009.

[3] *See, e.g., id.*

[4] U.S. CONST. Art. 1, § 2, cl. 3 ("Representatives and direct Taxes shall be apportioned among the several States which may be included within this Union, according to their respective Numbers, which shall be determined by adding to the whole Number of free Persons, including those bound to Service for a Term of Years, and excluding Indians not taxed, three fifths of all other Persons. The actual Enumeration shall be made within three Years after the first Meeting of the Congress of the United States, and within every subsequent Term of ten Years, in such Manner as they shall by Law direct ..."); Amend. XIV, § 2, cl. 1 ("Representatives shall be apportioned among the several States according to their respective numbers, counting the whole number of persons in each State, excluding Indians not taxed.").

[5] The Constitution also requires the census data be used to apportion direct taxes among the states, although the Sixteenth Amendment removes "taxes on income" from the requirement of apportionment. U.S. CONST. Art. 1, § 2, cl. 3; Amend. XVI. While the exact scope of direct taxes is unclear, the federal government does not currently impose any taxes subject to apportionment.

[6] U.S. CONST. Art. 1, § 2, cl. 3.

[7] 13 U.S.C. § 141.

[8] *See* U.S. Census Bureau, Population Division, *Census 2000: Plans and Rules for Taking the Census*, available at http://www.census.gov/population/

[9] *See id.*

[10] U.S. Census Bureau, *The Questions on the Form*, http://2010.census.gov/2010census/how/interactive-form.php.

[11] 13 U.S.C. § 5 ("The Secretary shall prepare questionnaires, and shall determine the inquiries, and the number, form, and subdivisions thereof, for the statistics, surveys, and censuses provided for in this title."); 13 U.S.C. § 141(a) ("The Secretary shall ... take a decennial census of population ... in such form and content as he may determine.... In connection with any such census, the Secretary is authorized to obtain such other census information as necessary."); 13 U.S.C. § 193 ("In advance of, in conjunction with, or after the taking of each census provided for by this chapter, the Secretary may make surveys and collect such preliminary and supplementary statistics related to the main topic of the census as are necessary to the initiation, taking, or completion thereof.").

[12] U.S. Census Bureau, *2009 American Community Survey*, http://www.census.gov/acs/www/Downloads/SQuest09.pdf.

[13] The earliest laws relating to immigration were laws providing for naturalization of foreign-born persons, prohibitions on the entry of certain types of aliens, such as criminals, and restrictions on the entry of foreign workers (specifically, the Chinese). The current framework for immigration was not established until the mid-twentieth century, so there would have been minimal basis for detailed information on immigration status. Currently, certain statistics concerning immigrant status may be collected and maintained by other federal agencies. The Department of Homeland Security maintains statistics regarding visa issuance. Nonimmigrant visa holders are permitted to enter and stay in the United States for limited periods; persons who enter as immigrants or who adjust their nonimmigrant status to lawful permanent resident status are permitted to remain in the United States indefinitely. Both the DHS and Executive Office of Immigration Review in the Department of Justice maintain statistics regarding grants of asylum. (Asylees may apply for lawful permanent resident status.) Statistics regarding unauthorized aliens have been published by various government agencies and non-governmental organizations, but are subject to debate and

dispute. For more information, see CRS Report RL33874, *Unauthorized Aliens Residing in the United States: Estimates Since 1986*, by Ruth Ellen Wasem.

[14]*See* Carroll D. Wright, *History and Grown of the U.S. Census, Prepared for the Senate Committee on the Census,* Department of Labor (1900), at 133, 139.

[15] *See, e.g., id.* at 147, 154 (censuses of 1850, 1860, and 1870).

[16] S.Amdt. 2635 ("none of the funds provided in this Act or any other act for any fiscal year may be used for collection of census data that does not include questions regarding United States citizenship and immigration status").

[17] U.S. CONST. Art. 1, § 2, cl. 3.

[18] As mentioned above, the ACS already asks for such information.

[19] Some commentators have argued there is no constitutional requirement that one class of aliens—illegal aliens—be counted for purposes of apportionment. *See, e.g.*, Charles Wood, *Losing Control of America's Future: The Census, Birthright Citizenship, and Illegal Aliens*, 22 HARV. J.L. & PUB. POL'Y 465 (1999)(arguing the Constitution permits a stricter test for residence than the Census Bureau's "usual residence" standard and does not require the counting of illegal aliens because they would not have the requisite stable inhabitancy in a state); *but see Note: A Territorial Approach to Representation for Illegal Aliens*, 80 MICH. L. REV. 1342 (1981-82)(arguing the Constitution, as evidenced by its language and history, requires illegal aliens be included).

[20] *See, e.g.,* U.S. CONST. Amend. I ("Congress shall make no law ... abridging ... the right of the people peaceably to assemble, and to petition the Government for a redress of grievances"); Amend. II ("A well regulated Militia, being necessary to the security of a free state, the right of the people to keep and bear Arms, shall not be infringed"); Amend. V ("No person shall be held to answer for a capital, or otherwise infamous crime, unless on a presentment or indictment of a Grand Jury ...").

[21] *See* Grosjean v. American Press Co., 297 U.S. 233, 244 (1936).

[22] *See, e.g.*, U.S. CONST. Art. I, § 2, cl. 2. ("No Person shall be a Representative who shall not have attained to the age of twenty five Years, and been seven Years a Citizen of the United States, and who shall not, when elected, be an Inhabitant of that State in which he shall be chosen.").

[23] *See, e.g.*, *Plyler v. Doe*, 457 U.S. 202, 210 (1982) ("Whatever his status under the immigration laws, an alien is surely a 'person' in any ordinary sense of that term. Aliens, even aliens whose presence in this country is unlawful, have long been recognized as 'persons' guaranteed due process of law by the Fifth and Fourteenth Amendments."). This does not mean that aliens must be afforded the same benefits as citizens. *See Matthew v. Diaz*, 426 U.S. 67, 78-79 (1976).

[24] While several cases have been brought challenging the inclusion of unauthorized aliens, courts have found the plaintiffs lacked standing to bring suit. *See Ridge v. Verity*, 715 F. Supp. 1308 (W.D. Penn. 1989); *Federation for American Immigration Reform (FAIR) v. Klutznick*, 486 F. Supp. 564 (D.D.C. 1980) (three-judge panel).

[25] *See FAIR*, 486 F. Supp. at 576 ("The language of the Constitution is not ambiguous. It requires the counting of the 'whole number of persons' for apportionment purposes, and while illegal aliens were not a component of the population at the time the Constitution was adopted, they are clearly 'persons.'").

[26] It could be argued that the treatment of women and children should not be compared to that of unauthorized aliens who are violating the laws of the United States. On the other hand, if the purpose of the census is understood to be counting all individuals who are actually inhabitants of the United States, then the comparison would be appropriate.

[27] Article I, § 2, cl. 1 provides that the voter qualifications in each state for those electing Representatives shall be the qualifications required by state laws for voters electing the most numerous branch of the State legislatures. Historically, some states extended the franchise for electing the most numerous branch of the state legislatures to lawful aliens for all elections. *See The Constitution of the United States of America: Analysis and Interpretation*, S. Doc. No. 108-17 283, fn. 1220 and accompanying text (2002); Jamin B. Raskin, *Legal Aliens, Local Citizens: the Historical, Constitutional and Theoretical Meanings of Alien Suffrage*, 141 U. PA. L. REV. 1391 (1993). Although today no state extends the franchise to aliens generally, some states do permit lawful permanent residents to vote in certain local elections, such as school board elections. The rationale appears to be that lawful residents have all the obligations of local residents, such as local property tax payments, and may have children attending local schools who are either lawful permanent residents or U.S. citizens themselves; therefore, they should be permitted to vote in certain local elections.

[28] *See Note, supra* note 18, at 1354. /www/censusdata/resid_rules.html

[29] *See id.* at 1354-55.

[30] *See FAIR*, 486 F. Supp. at 576.

[31] *See* M. Farrand, *The Records of the Federal Convention of 1787*, vol. 2, at 571, 590-91.

[32] *See FAIR*, 486 F. Supp. at 576 (citing The Federalist, No. 54, at 369 (J. Cooke ed. 1961)).

[33] *See* CONG. GLOBE, 39th CONG., 1st Sess. 357-59, 2986-87 (1866).

[34] *See id.* at 359 (statement by Rep. Conkling); *see also id.* at 2986-87 (statement by Sen. Wilson).

[35] *Id.* at 359 (statement by Rep. Conkling).

[36] *See Note, supra* note 19, at 1356 (citing to James, *The Framing of the Fourteenth Amendment*, 37 ILL. STUD. SOC. SCI. 3, 195-96 (1956)).

[37] *See, e.g.*, H.J. Res. 20, 101, 263, 356, 484, 71st Cong. (1931); S. 2366, 96th Cong. (1980).

[38] *See, e.g.*, 86 Cong. Rec. 4371-72 (1940)(remarks by Rep. Celler asserting that the term "persons" refers to all individuals, including aliens who are in the country unlawfully); *1980 Census: Counting Illegal Aliens, Hearings on S. 2366 Before the Subcomm. on Governmental Affairs*, 96th Cong. 12 (1980) (statement by Sen. Javits asserting that the Constitution requires counting all aliens for apportionment purposes).

[39] U.S. CONST. Art I, §8, cl. 4 ("The Congress shall have Power ... To establish an uniform Rule of Naturalization ...").

[40] *See Note, supra* note 19, at 1345-48.

[41] *See* Dennis L. Murphy, *Note: The Exclusion of Illegal Aliens From the Reapportionment Base: A Question of Representation*, 41 Case W. Res. 969, 985-86 (1991).

[42] *Wesberry v. Sanders*, 376 U.S. 1 (1964).

[43] *See* Murphy, *supra* note 41.

[44] This distinction is important because the Constitution only requires the use of census data for apportionment among the states, not for redistricting and reapportionment within them. Thus, states can determine what data shall be used for redistricting within a state. This issue is discussed further in the next section.

[45] *See Wisconsin v. City of New York*, 517 U.S. 1, 13-15 (1996); *Dept. of Commerce v. Montana*, 503 U.S. 442, 461-63 (1992); *see also FAIR*, 486 F. Supp. at 577.

[46] *Dept. of Commerce*, 503 U.S. at 463.

[47] *Id.*

[48] *See FAIR*, 486 F. Supp. at 577; *see also Note, supra* note 19, at 1358-63.

[49]*See* Carroll D. Wright, *History and Grown of the U.S. Census, Prepared for the Senate Committee on the Census,* Department of Labor (1900), at 133, 139.

[50] *See, e.g., id.* at 147, 154 (censuses of 1850, 1860, and 1870).

[51] *See id.* at 135, 140-41 (reprinting instructions to the Marshals for the 1820 and 1830 censuses).

[52] *See Kirkpatrick v. Preisler,* 394 U.S. 526 (1969) (court indicated in dicta that the use of projected population figures was not per se unconstitutional and that states may properly consider such statistical data if such data would have a high degree of accuracy); *Senate of the State of California v. Mosbacher*, 968 F.2d 974 (9th Cir. 1992) (court noted that if a state knows that census data is underrepresentative of the population, it can and should utilize non-census data, in addition to the official count, for redistricting); *Young v. Klutznick*, 652 F.2d 617, 624 (6th Cir. 1981) (in dicta, the court stated that the state legislature is not required by the federal Constitution to use census data supplied by the Census Bureau for congressional redistricting, but could use adjusted population figures when redistricting between decennial censuses, as long as the adjustment is thoroughly documented and applied in a systematic manner*); City of Detroit v. Franklin*, 800 F. Supp. 539, 543 (E.D. Mich. 1992) (court held that an earlier Supreme Court case did not find that states must use census figures in redistricting; rather, the Supreme Court had "merely reiterated a well-established rule of constitutional law: states are required to use the 'best census data available' or 'the best population data available' in their attempts to effect proportionate political representation").

[53] 394 U.S. 526 (1969).

[54] 384 U.S. 73, 91 (1966).

[55] 384 U.S. at 93.

[56] *See also MacGovern v. Connolly*, 637 F. Supp. 111 (D. Mass. 1986) (court upheld state redistricting scheme which entailed use of data from a decennial state census held every 10 years beginning in 1975 and refused to order a new scheme based on "inapposite" 1980 federal census data); *Klahr v. Williams*, 313 F. Supp. 148 (D. Ariz. 1970) (court held invalid congressional and state legislative redistricting plans based, *inter alia*, on a population estimate formula "converting 1968 voter registration to 1960 census on a proportionate basis" which did not truly represent the population, but ordered the plan used anyway because no better alternative was feasible before the next election).

[57] 918 F.2d 763, 773-776 (9th Cir. 1990), *cert. denied*, 498 U.S. 1028 (1991).

[58] 532 U.S. 1046 (2001).

[59] *Id.* (citing *Chen v. City of Houston*, 206 F.3d 502 (5th Cir. 2000)(looking to Supreme Court precedent, *Burns v. Richardson*, 384 U.S. 73, 92 (1966), for the proposition that "the choice between measurements 'involves choices about the nature of representation with which we have been shown no constitutionally founded reason to interfere.'"); *Daly v. Hunt*, 93 F.3d 1212, 1227 (4th Cir. 1996)(finding "[t]here is no reason to believe that voting-age population is significantly better than total population in achieving the goal of one person, one vote" and until the Supreme Court speaks clearly on this issue, any actions by the courts "[should be] tempered by the overriding theme in the Court's prior apportionment cases weighing against judicial involvement.")).

[60] The issue of what constitutes official federal decennial census data was considered during the oral arguments in the census sampling cases. Oral Argument Transcript, found at 1998 WL 827383 on Westlaw (oral argument of Michael A. Carvin on behalf of the appellees in No. 98-564) (discussing what data states would use if adjusted and unadjusted data sets were released).

[61] 525 U.S. at 332-4, 119 S. Ct. at 774-5.

[62] *See, e.g.*, the following legislation enacted in Alaska, Arizona, Colorado, Kansas, and Virginia. In Alaska, S.B. 99, Ch. 18 of the 1999 Acts, was enacted on May 11, 1999. In Arizona, H.B. 2698, Ch. 47 of the 1999 Laws, was enacted on April 22, 1999. In Colorado, S.B. 206, Ch. 170 of the 1999 Laws, was enacted on May 7, 1999. In Kansas, S.B. 351, Ch. 148 of the 1999 Laws, was enacted on May 12, 1999. In Virginia, H.B. 1486, ch. 884 of the 2000 Acts, was enacted on April 9, 2000.

[63] Until 1929, the statutes implementing each decennial census were enacted prior to each census. The Census Act of 1954 superseded the 1929 statute; census legislation since 1954 has generally taken the form of amendments to the 1954 statute.

[64] Act of March 1, 1790, 1st Cong., Stat. 101. C.D. Wright, *History and Growth of the United States Census* (1900) [hereinafter *History*], pp. 132-133, 925-927.

[65] Reprinted in C.D. Wright, *History*, *supra* note 64, at 135.

[66] 36, pt. 1, Cong. Globe 351-359 (Jan. 22, 1866).

[67] 36, pt. 1, Cong. Globe 141-142 (Jan. 8, 1866).

[68] C.E. Turney, Law Assistant, Senate Legislative Counsel, *Power of Congress to Exclude Aliens from Enumeration for Purposes of Apportionment of Representatives* (April 30, 1929), reprinted at 71 Cong. Rec. 1821 (May 23, 1929).

[69] *E.g.*, H. J. Res. 356, 71st Cong. (1931), proposing to amend the Constitution of the United States to exclude aliens in counting the whole number of persons in each state for apportionment of Representatives among the several states; reported with amendments in H. Rept. 71-2761 and considered at 74 Cong. Rec. 5454 (Feb. 19, 1931).

[70] 86 Cong. Rec. 4372 (April 11, 1940).

[71] *E.g.*, H.R. 6769, S. 2366, 96th Cong., and H.J.Res. 199, S. 358, §601, 101st Cong. (1989).

[72] Senate-passed version of H.R. 2991, 101st Cong. (1989).

[73] S. 358, §601, 101st Cong. (1989).

[74] 135 Cong. Rec. H 6952 (October 11, 1989) (appointment of conferees on H.R. 2991, Departments of Commerce, Justice, and State, the Judiciary, and Related Agencies Appropriations Act, 1990). The House of Representatives voted down similar amendments for H.R. 2991 before going to conference on the bill. The conference version did not include the Senate language; the Senate conferees agreed to deletion of this language. H. Rep't. 101-299 at 87 (1990) (discussing Amdt. No. 188, deletion of Senate language that would have prohibited the counting of illegal aliens in the census for apportionment).

The House of Representatives... ISBN: 978-1-61324-308-4
Editors: R. D. Orsino, O. G. Trance

Chapter 10

DISTRICT OF COLUMBIA REPRESENTATION: EFFECT ON HOUSE APPORTIONMENT*

Royce Crocker

SUMMARY

Two proposals (H.R. 157 / S. 160) have been introduced in the 111th Congress to provide for voting representation in the U.S. House of Representatives for the residents of the District of Columbia (DC). H.R. 157 /S. 160, for purposes of voting representation, treat the District of Columbia as if it were a state, giving a House seat to the District, but restricting it to a single seat under any future apportionments. The bills also would increase the size of the House to 437 members from 435, and give the additional seat to the state of Utah. This report shows the distribution of House seats based on the 2000 census for 435 seats and for 437 seats as specified in the proposal. The report also examines the impact of using the 2009 estimated population to allocate the 437 seats, including the single seat provided to the District in the 2010 reapportionment.

* This is an edited, reformatted and augmented version of a Congressional Research Services publication, dated January 29, 2010.

BACKGROUND

H.R. 157 / S. 160, the District of Columbia House Voting Rights Act of 2009, would provide for a permanent increase in the size of the U.S. House of Representatives, from 435 seats to 437 seats.[1] The bills specify that one of the seats is to be allocated to the District of Columbia while the other seat is to be assigned either by using the normal apportionment formula allocation procedure (H.R. 157) or specifying that the seat would be allocated to Utah, thus adding a fourth seat (S. 160). While both versions treat the District of Columbia as if it were a state for the purposes of the allocation of House seats, each restricts the District of Columbia to a single congressional seat under any future apportionments.

Similar bills were introduced in the 110th Congress. On April 19, 2007, the House approved H.R. 1905 (a revised version of H.R. 1433) by a vote of 241 to 177 (Roll Call vote 231) and sent it to the Senate for consideration. On June 28, 2007, S. 1257 was reported out of the Senate Committee on Homeland Security and Governmental Affairs with amendments. On September 18, 2007, cloture on the motion to proceed to consideration of the measure was not invoked in the Senate on a Yea-Nay vote, 57 - 42, leaving the measure pending. No further action occurred on the legislation.

ADDING NEW STATES AND SEATS TO THE HOUSE

The 435 seat limit for the size of the House was imposed in 1929 by statute (46 Stat. 21, 26-27). Altering the size of the House would require a new law setting a different limit. Article I, §2 of the Constitution establishes a minimum House size (one Representative for each state), and a maximum House size (one for every 30,000 persons, or 9,380 representatives based on the 2000 Census). In 2003, a House size of 473 would have resulted in no state losing seats held from the 103rd to the 107th Congresses. However, by retaining seats through an increase in the House size, other state delegations would become larger. At a House size of 473, California's delegation size, for example, would be 57 instead of 53 seats.

Congressional Precedent

General congressional practice when admitting new states to the Union has been to increase the size of the House, either permanently or temporarily, to accommodate the new states. New states usually resulted in *additions* to the size of the House in the 19th and early 20th centuries. The exceptions to this general rule occurred when states were formed from other states (Maine, Kentucky, and West Virginia). These states' Representatives came from the allocations of Representatives of the states from which the new ones had been formed.

When Alaska and Hawaii were admitted in 1959 and 1960 the House size was *temporarily* increased to 437. This modern precedent differed from the state admission acts passed following the censuses in the 19th and early 20th centuries which provided that new state representatives would be added to the apportionment totals.

The apportionment act of 1911 anticipated the admission of Arizona and New Mexico by providing for an increase in the House size from 433 to 435 if the states were admitted.

As noted above, the House size was temporarily increased to 437 to accommodate Alaska and Hawaii in 1960. In 1961, when the President reported the 1960 census results and the resulting reapportionment of seats in the reestablished 435-seat House, Alaska was entitled to one seat, and Hawaii to two seats. Massachusetts, Pennsylvania and Missouri each received one less seat than they would have if the House size had been increased to 438 (as was proposed by H.R. 10264, in 1962).

Reapportionment Impact

Table 1 lists the actual apportionment allocations of Representatives based on the 2000 census for 435 seats and the apportionment that would occur as a result of the provisions of the proposed legislation (i.e., 437 seats, DC allocated a seat and Utah allocated a seat). In addition, a projection of the 2010 apportionment of 437 seats for the House of Representatives is shown based on 2000- 2009 state population estimates and providing for a seat for the District of Columbia.

If the District of Columbia had been treated as a state in the reapportionment of congressional seats following the 2000 census, and the House size had remained at 435, North Carolina would not have gained an additional seat in comparison with the 1990s. The state's delegation would have remained at 12 Representatives.

If the District of Columbia were to receive representation as if it were a state and the House size were to be increased to 437, DC would be entitled to one Representative and Utah would be entitled to four Representatives, one more than the state received in the reapportionment following the 2000 census. No other state would be affected by the change. This is the impact that the proponents of the proposed legislation hope to achieve.

If either of the pending bills are enacted and 2000-2009 estimates of the 2010 population of the states are used as a projection for what might happen in the 2010 apportionment, the District would get its seat and Utah would retain its fourth seat. Georgia, Nevada, and South Carolina would each pick up a seat, Arizona and Florida would pick up two seats and Texas would be allocated an additional three seats. Illinois, Iowa, Louisiana, Massachusetts, Michigan, New Jersey, New York, and Pennsylvania would each lose a single seat, while Ohio would lose two seats. These changes are primarily due to estimated changes in state populations since the 2000 census.

The actual apportionment is done through a "priority list" calculated using the equal proportions formula provided in 2 U.S.C. §2a.(a). *Table 2* displays the end of the priority list that was used to allocate Representatives based on the 2000 Census. The law only provides for 435 seats in the House, but the tables illustrate not only the last seats assigned by the apportionment formula (ending at 435), but the states that would just miss getting additional representation.[2]

Table 3 is similar to *Table 2*, in that it displays the end of the priority list, but the last seat is 437 instead of 435. The priority values and the population needed to gain or lose a seat do not change if DC is treated like state, as DC is entitled the constitutional minimum of one Representative.

Table 1. Apportionment Impact of Alternative Plans for DC Voting Representation in the House

Actual 2000 Allocation: 435 Representatives			437 Representatives							
			DC Given Own Seat				DC Given Own Seat			
ST	Apportionment Pop.	Seats	ST	2000 Apportionment Pop.[b]	Seats	Seat Change from 2000	ST	2010 Projected Population Based on 2000-2009 Estimates[c]	Seats	Seat Change from 2000
AL	4,461,130	7	AL	4,461,130	7		AL	4,722,033	7	
AK	628,933	1	AK	628,933	1		AK	706,757	1	
AZ	5,140,683	8	AZ	5,140,683	8		AZ	6,816,325	10	+2
AR	2,679,733	4	AR	2,679,733	4		AR	2,911,097	4	
CA	33,930,798	53	CA	33,930,798	53		CA	37,255,448	53	
CO	4,311,882	7	CO	4,311,882	7		CO	5,067,957	7	
CT	3,409,535	5	CT	3,409,535	5		CT	3,528,228	5	
DCa	574,096	0	DC	574,096	1	+1	DC	897,619	1	+1
DE	785,068	1	DE	785,068	1		DE	595,925	1	
FL	16,028,890	25	FL	16,028,890	25		FL	19,075,858	27	+2
GA	8,206,975	13	GA	8,206,975	13		GA	10,038,872	14	+1
HI	1,216,642	2	HI	1,216,642	2		HI	1,308,549	2	
ID	1,297,274	2	ID	1,297,274	2		ID	1,577,524	2	
IL	12,439,042	19	IL	12,439,042	19		IL	12,937,086	18	-1
IN	6,090,782	9	IN	6,090,782	9		IN	6,454,439	9	
IA	2,931,923	5	IA	2,931,923	5		IA	3,006,181	4	-1
KS	2,693,824	4	KS	2,693,824	4		KS	2,819,278	4	

Table 1. (Continued).

Actual 2000 Allocation: 435 Representatives			437 Representatives							
			DC Given Own Seat				DC Given Own Seat			
ST	Apportion-ment Pop.	Seats	ST	2000 Apportion-ment Pop.[b]	Seats	Seat Change from 2000	ST	2010 Projected Population Based on 2000-2009 Estimates[c]	Seats	Seat Change from 2000
KY	4,049,431	6	KY	4,049,431	6		KY	4,342,913	6	
LA	4,480,271	7	LA	4,480,271	7		LA	4,408,371	6	-1
ME	1,277,731	2	ME	1,277,731	2		ME	1,330,583	2	
MD	5,307,886	8	MD	5,307,886	8		MD	5,763,312	8	
MA	6,355,568	10	MA	6,355,568	10		MA	6,578,643	9	-1
MI	9,955,829	15	MI	9,955,829	15		MI	10,042,335	14	-1
MN	4,925,670	8	MN	4,925,670	8		MN	5,297,832	8	
MS	2,852,927	4	MS	2,852,927	4		MS	2,957,828	4	
MO	5,606,260	9	MO	5,606,260	9		MO	6,034,391	9	
MT	905,316	1	MT	905,316	1		MT	981,446	1	
NE	1,715,369	3	NE	1,715,369	3		NE	1,799,668	3	
NV	2,002,032	3	NV	2,002,032	3		NV	2,761,669	4	+1
NH	1,238,415	2	NH	1,238,415	2		NH	1,343,413	2	
NJ	8,424,354	13	NJ	8,424,354	13		NJ	8,734,543	12	-1
NM	1,823,821	3	NM	1,823,821	3		NM	2,029,960	3	
NY	19,004,973	29	NY	19,004,973	29		NY	19,598,281	28	-1
NCa	8,067,673	13	NC	8,067,673	13		NC	9,485,781	13	
ND	643,756	1	ND	643,756	1		ND	641,905	1	
OH	11,374,540	18	OH	11,374,540	18		OH	11,571,055	16	-2
OK	3,458,819	5	OK	3,458,819	5		OK	3,687,874	5	
OR	3,428,543	5	OR	3,428,543	5		OR	3,859,470	5	
PA	12,300,670	19	PA	12,300,670	19		PA	12,627,120	18	-1

RI	1,049,662	2	RI	1,049,662	2		RI	1,056,962	2	
SC	4,025,061	6	SC	4,025,061	6		SC	4,600,842	7	+1
SD	756,874	1	SD	756,874	1		SD	815,863	1	
TN	5,700,037	9	TN	5,700,037	9		TN	6,361,597	9	
TX	20,903,994	32	TX	20,903,994	32		TX	25,098,728	36	+3
UT	2,236,714	3	UT	2,236,714	4	+1	UT	2,835,918	4	+1
VT	609,890	1	VT	609,890	1		VT	624,294	1	
VA	7,100,702	11	VA	7,100,702	11		VA	7,980,639	11	
WA	5,908,684	9	WA	5,908,684	9		WA	6,715,594	9	
WV	1,813,077	3	WV	1,813,077	3		WV	1,816,881	3	
WI	5,371,210	8	WI	5,371,210	8		WI	5,693,015	8	
WY	495,304	1	WY	495,304	1		WY	540,885	1	
		435			437				437	

Note: All apportionment calculations by CRS using the "method of equal proportions" formula mandated by 2 U.S.C. §2a.(a).

a If DC had been allocated representatives as if it were a state after the 2000 Census it would have been entitled to one representative, and North Carolina would have received 12 instead of 13.

bThe apportionment population is different from the actual resident population of each state because the Census Bureau adds to each state's resident population the foreign-based military and other federal employees and their dependents who are from the state but not residing therein at the time of the census.

c Source: http://www.census.gov/popest/datasets.html, Population Change: April 1, 2000 to July 1, 2009 (NSTEST2009). Site last visited, January 29, 2010.

Table 2. Population Needed to Gain or Lose a Seat Using the 2000 Census Apportionment Population and a 435 Seat House

Priority	State	Seat	2000 Apportionment Population	Priority Value[a]	Pop. Needed to[b] Gain or Lose Seat
425	PA	19	12,300,670	665,144.05	-359,885
426	TX	32	20,903,994	663,702.45	-567,519
427	MO	9	5,606,260	660,703.78	-127,450
428	CA	52	33,930,798	658,881.42	-679,651
429	MN	8	4,925,670	658,220.10	-93,814
430	GA	13	8,206,975	657,083.72	-142,386
431	IA	5	2,931,923	655,597.81	-44,337
432	FL	25	16,028,890	654,376.65	-212,933
433	OH	18	11,374,540	650,239.14	-79,688
434	CA	53	33,930,798	646,330.20	-33,940
435	NC	13	8,067,673	645,930.64	-3,084
			Last seat assigned by law		
436	UT	4	2,236,714	645,683.70	+855
437	NY	30	19,004,973	644,328.90	+47,245
438	TX	33	20,903,994	643,275.93	+86,268
439	MI	16	9,955,829	642,645.62	+50,891
440	IN	10	6,090,782	642,024.48	+37,057
441	MT	2	905,316	640,155.07	+8,168
442	IL	20	12,439,042	638,109.37	+152,465
443	MS	5	2,852,927	637,933.77	+35,763
444	CA	54	33,930,798	634,248.18	+624,984
445	WI	9	5,371,210	633,002.89	+109,696
446	OK	6	3,458,819	631,490.94	+79,090
447	PA	20	12,300,670	631,011.04	+290,837
448	FL	26	16,028,890	628,704.74	+439,176
449	OR	6	3,428,543	625,963.33	+109,365
450	MD	9	5,307,886	625,540.08	+173,020

Source: Computations of priority values and populations needed to gain or lose a seat by CRS. See CRS Report RL30711, *The House Apportionment Formula in Theory and Practice*, by Royce Crocker, for an explanation of formula for allocating House seats.

a Each state's claim to representation in the House is based on a "priority value" determined by the following formula: $PV = P / [n(n - 1)]^{1/2}$; where PV = the state's priority value, P = the state's population, and n = the state's nth seat in the House. For example, the priority value of Wisconsin's 9th seat is:

$PVWI9 = 5{,}371{,}210 / [9(9 - 1)]^{1/2}$

$= 5{,}371{,}210 / [72]^{1/2}$

$= 5{,}371{,}210 / 8.485281374238570 = 633{,}002.89$

The actual seat assignments are made by ranking all of the states' priority values from highest to lowest until 435 seats are allocated.

b These figures represent the population a state would either need to lose in order to drop below the 435th seat cutoff, or to gain to rise above the cutoff. If, in the case of Wisconsin, 109,696 more persons had been counted in the Census, the state's priority value would have been increased to 645,930.77 which would have resulted in a new sequence number of 435 because North Carolina's 13th seat would have occupied the 436th position in the priority list.

Table 3. Population Needed to Gain or Lose a Seat Using the 2000 Census Apportionment Population and a 437 Seat House

Priority	State	Seat	2000 Apportionment Population	Priority Value	Pop. Needed to Gain or Lose Seat
425	CO	7	4,311,882	665,337.67	-136,152
426	PA	19	12,300,670	665,144.05	-384,940
427	TX	32	20,903,994	663,702.45	-610,190
428	MO	9	5,606,260	660,703.78	-138,946
429	CA	52	33,930,798	658,881.42	-749,420
430	MN	8	4,925,670	658,220.10	-103,952
431	GA	13	8,206,975	657,083.72	-159,308
432	IA	5	2,931,923	655,597.81	-50,396
433	FL	25	16,028,890	654,376.65	-246,119
434	OH	18	11,374,540	650,239.14	-103,387
435	CA	53	33,930,798	646,330.20	-105,063
436	NC	13	8,067,673	645,930.64	-20,006
437	UT	4	2,236,714	645,683.70	-4,693
Last seat assigned under proposal					
438	NY	30	19,004,973	644,328.90	+39,961
439	TX	33	20,903,994	643,275.93	+78,243
440	MI	16	9,955,829	642,645.62	+47,066
441	IN	10	6,090,782	642,024.48	+34,714
442	MT	2	905,316	640,155.07	+7,819
443	IL	20	12,439,042	638,109.37	+147,651
444	MS	5	2,852,927	637,933.77	+34,659
445	CA	54	33,930,798	634,248.18	+611,774
446	WI	9	5,371,210	633,002.89	+107,600
447	OK	6	3,458,819	631,490.94	+77,737
448	PA	20	12,300,670	631,011.04	+286,023
449	FL	26	16,028,890	628,704.74	+432,880
450	OR	6	3,428,543	625,963.33	+108,013

See notes end of Table 2.

End Notes

[1] See CRS Report RL33830, District of Columbia Voting Representation in Congress: An Analysis of Legislative Proposals, by Eugene Boyd for a complete discussion.

[2] The figures in Table 2 for the "population needed to gain or lose a seat" are misleading because it is unlikely that one state's population total would be adjusted without others changing as well. Since the method of equal proportions used to allocate seats in the House uses all state populations simultaneously, changes in several state populations may also result in changes to the "populations needed to gain or lose a seat."

The House of Representatives... ISBN: 978-1-61324-308-4
Editors: R. D. Orsino, O. G. Trance

Chapter 11

PUERTO RICAN STATEHOOD: EFFECTS ON HOUSE APPORTIONMENT*

Royce Crocker

SUMMARY

For years, the people of the Commonwealth of Puerto Rico have been involved in discussions relating to changing the political status of Puerto Rico from a commonwealth of the United States to either the 51st state or an independent nation, or maintaining the status quo as a commonwealth.

In the 111th Congress, H.R. 2499, introduced by Representative Pedro Pierluisi, would establish procedures to determine Puerto Rico's political status. It would authorize a two-stage plebiscite in Puerto Rico to reconsider the status issue. H.R. 2499 is similar to H.R. 900 as introduced in the 110th Congress. A possible outcome of this process is Puerto Rican statehood.

Proposals to change Puerto Rico's governmental relationship with the United States from a commonwealth to some other model raise many political, social, and economic issues. This report focuses exclusively on what impact adding a new state that is more populous than 24 of the existing 50 states would have on representation in the House of Representatives.

---

* This is an edited, reformatted and augmented version of a Congressional Research Services publication, dated March 11, 2010.

Statehood for Puerto Rico would likely cause Congress to explore whether the current limit of 435 seats in the House of Representatives should be changed. If Puerto Rico had been a state when the 2000 census was taken, it would have been entitled to six Representatives based on its 2000 census population of 3.8 million residents. Based on current estimates of almost 4 million residents, Puerto Rico would still be entitled to six Representatives if it were to become a state today.

If the House were faced with the addition of six new Representatives, it could accommodate them either by expanding the size of the House or adhering to the current 435-seat statutory limit, which would reduce the number of Representatives in other states.

Introduction and Background

In the 111th Congress, H.R. 2499, introduced by Representative Pedro Pierluisi, would establish procedures to determine Puerto Rico's political status. It would authorize a two-stage plebiscite in Puerto Rico to reconsider the status issue. H.R. 2499 is similar to H.R. 900 as introduced in the 110th Congress. A possible outcome of this process is Puerto Rican statehood.

If Puerto Rico's citizens vote in favor of statehood in the series of plebiscites as outlined in H.R. 2499, then Puerto Rico would, most likely, be entitled to six Representatives in the House of Representatives as well as two United States Senators. If the size of the House remains fixed at the legally mandated 435-seat limit, then six states would likely have one fewer Representatives than they would have had if Puerto Rico had not become a state. Another option that the House could choose given the entrance of another state is to increase the size of the House.

Apportionment Options when Admitting New States

Congressional Precedent

General congressional practice when admitting new states to the union has been to increase the size of the House, either permanently or temporarily, to accommodate the new states. New states usually resulted in additions to the size of the House in the 19th and early 20th centuries. The exceptions to this general rule occurred when states were formed from other states (Maine,

Kentucky, and West Virginia). These states' Representatives came from the allocations of Representatives of the states from which the new ones had been formed.[1]

When Alaska and Hawaii were admitted in 1959 and 1960 the House size was temporarily increased to 437. This modern precedent differed from the state admission acts passed following the censuses in the 19th and early 20th centuries, which provided that new states' representation would be added to the apportionment totals. *Table 1* lists the number of seats each state has received after each census, and the notes show the initial seat assignments to states admitted between censuses.

The apportionment act of 1911 anticipated the admission of Arizona and New Mexico by providing for an increase in the House size from 433 to 435 if the states were admitted. And, as noted above, the House size was temporarily increased to 437 to accommodate Alaska and Hawaii in 1960.

In 1961, when the President reported the 1960 census results and the resulting reapportionment of seats in the reestablished 435-seat House, Alaska was entitled to one seat, and Hawaii two seats. Massachusetts, Pennsylvania, and Missouri each received one less seat than they would have if the House size had been increased to 438 (as was proposed by H.R. 10264, in 1962).

Puerto Rican Statehood Apportionment Options

If Puerto Rico were admitted to statehood between censuses, Congress would have at least three options for handling the approximately six Representatives the new state would be entitled to under the current apportionment formula: (1) subtract seats from states that would have lost them if Puerto Rico had been admitted before the previous census; (2) temporarily increase the size of the House until the next census; or (3) permanently increase the size of the House.

The first option, subtracting seats from other states, has only been done by Congress when new states were formed from existing states. This would require the losing states to redistrict to account for these losses. The second option, temporarily increasing the House size, has only been done once, in the Alaska and Hawaii precedent. The third option, permanently increasing the House size (probably to 441), was the procedure commonly used in the 19th and early 20th centuries.

Table 1. Representatives Under Each Apportionment 1789-2000

ST	1789	1790	1800	1810	1820	1830	1840	1850	1860	1870	1880	1890	1900	1910	1920	1930	1940	1950	1960	1970	1980	1990	2000
AL	NA	NA	NA	1	3	5	7	7	6	8	8	9	9	10	10	9	9	9	8	7	7	7	7
AK	NA	NA	NA	NA	NA	NA	NA	NA	NA	NA	NA	NA	NA	NA	NA	NA	NA	1	1	1	1	1	1
AZ	NA	NA	NA	NA	NA	NA	NA	NA	NA	NA	NA	NA	NA	1	1	1	2	2	3	4	5	6	8
AR	NA	NA	NA	NA	NA	1	1	2	3	4	5	6	7	7	7	7	7	6	4	4	4	4	4
CA	NA	NA	NA	NA	NA	NA	2	2	3	4	6	7	8	11	11	20	23	30	38	43	45	52	53
CO	NA	NA	NA	NA	NA	NA	NA	NA	NA	1	1	2	3	4	4	4	4	4	4	5	6	6	7
CT	5	7	7	7	6	6	4	4	4	4	4	4	5	5	5	6	6	6	6	6	6	6	5
DE	1	1	1	2	1	1	1	1	1	1	1	1	1	1	1	1	1	1	1	1	1	1	1
FL	NA	NA	NA	NA	NA	NA	1	1	1	2	2	2	3	4	4	5	6	8	12	15	19	23	25
GA	3	2	4	6	7	9	8	8	7	9	10	11	11	12	12	10	10	10	10	10	10	11	13
HI	NA	NA	NA	NA	NA	NA	NA	NA	NA	NA	NA	NA	NA	NA	NA	NA	NA	1	2	2	2	2	2
ID	NA	NA	NA	NA	NA	NA	NA	NA	NA	NA	1	1	1	2	2	2	2	2	2	2	2	2	2
IL	NA	NA	NA	1	1	3	7	9	14	19	20	22	25	27	27	27	26	25	24	24	22	20	19
IN	NA	NA	NA	1	3	7	10	11	11	13	13	13	13	13	13	12	11	11	11	11	10	10	9
IA	NA	NA	NA	NA	NA	NA	2	2	6	9	11	11	11	11	11	9	8	8	7	6	6	5	5
KS	NA	NA	NA	NA	NA	NA	NA	NA	1	3	7	8	8	8	8	7	6	6	5	5	5	4	4
KY	NA	2	6	10	12	13	10	10	9	10	11	11	11	11	11	9	9	8	7	7	7	6	6
ST	1789	1790	1800	1810	1820	1830	1840	1850	1860	1870	1880	1890	1900	1910	1920	1930	1940	1950	1960	1970	1980	1990	2000
LA	NA	NA	NA	1	3	3	4	4	5	6	6	6	7	8	8	8	8	8	8	8	8	7	7
ME	NA	NA	NA	NA	7	8	7	6	5	5	4	4	4	4	4	3	3	3	2	2	2	2	2
MD	6	8	9	9	9	8	6	6	5	6	6	6	6	6	6	6	6	7	8	8	8	8	8
MA	8	14	17	20	13	12	10	11	10	11	12	13	14	16	16	15	14	14	12	12	11	10	10
MI	NA	NA	NA	NA	NA	1	3	4	6	9	11	12	12	13	13	17	17	18	19	19	18	16	15
MN	NA	NA	NA	NA	NA	NA	NA	2	2	3	5	7	9	10	10	9	9	9	8	8	8	8	8
MS	NA	NA	NA	1	1	2	4	5	5	6	7	7	8	8	8	7	7	6	5	5	5	5	4
MO	NA	NA	NA	NA	1	2	5	7	9	13	14	15	16	16	16	13	13	11	10	10	9	9	9
MT	NA	NA	NA	NA	NA	NA	NA	NA	NA	NA	1	1	1	2	2	2	2	2	2	2	2	1	1
NE	NA	NA	NA	NA	NA	NA	NA	NA	1	1	3	6	6	6	6	5	4	4	3	3	3	3	3
NV	NA	NA	NA	NA	NA	NA	NA	NA	1	1	1	1	1	1	1	1	1	1	1	1	2	2	3
NH	3	4	5	6	6	5	4	3	3	3	2	2	2	2	2	2	2	2	2	2	2	2	2
NJ	4	5	6	6	6	6	5	5	5	7	7	8	10	12	12	14	14	14	15	15	14	13	13

Table 1. (Continued).

NM	NA	NA	NA	NA	NA	NA	NA	NA	NA	NA	NA	NA	NA	1	1	1	2	2	2	2	3	3	3
NY	6	10	17	27	34	40	34	33	31	33	33	34	37	43	43	45	45	43	41	39	34	31	29
NC	5	10	12	13	13	13	9	8	7	8	9	9	10	10	10	11	12	12	11	11	11	12	13
ND	NA	NA	NA	NA	NA	NA	NA	NA	NA	NA	1	1	2	3	3	2	2	2	2	1	1	1	1
OH	NA	NA	1	6	14	19	21	21	19	20	21	21	21	22	22	24	23	23	24	23	21	19	18
ST	1789	1790	1800	1810	1820	1830	1840	1850	1860	1870	1880	1890	1900	1910	1920	1930	1940	1950	1960	1970	1980	1990	2000
OK	NA	NA	NA	NA	NA	NA	NA	NA	NA	NA	NA	NA	5	8	8	9	8	6	6	6	6	6	5
OR	NA	NA	NA	NA	NA	NA	NA	1	1	1	1	2	2	3	3	3	4	4	4	4	5	5	5
PA	8	13	18	23	26	28	24	25	24	27	28	30	32	36	36	34	33	30	27	25	23	21	19
RI	1	2	2	2	2	2	2	2	2	2	2	2	2	3	3	2	2	2	2	2	2	2	2
SC	5	6	8	9	9	9	7	6	4	5	7	7	7	7	7	6	6	6	6	6	6	6	6
SD	NA	NA	NA	NA	NA	NA	NA	NA	NA	NA	2	2	2	3	3	2	2	2	2	2	1	1	1
TN	NA	1	3	6	9	13	11	10	8	10	10	10	10	10	10	9	10	9	9	8	9	9	9
TX	NA	NA	NA	NA	NA	NA	2	2	4	6	11	13	16	18	18	21	21	22	23	24	27	30	32
UT	NA	NA	NA	NA	NA	NA	NA	NA	NA	NA	NA	1	1	2	2	2	2	2	2	2	3	3	3
VT	NA	2	4	6	5	5	4	3	3	3	2	2	2	2	2	1	1	1	1	1	1	1	1
VA	10	19	22	23	22	21	15	13	11	9	10	10	10	10	10	9	9	10	10	10	10	11	11
WA	NA	NA	NA	NA	NA	NA	NA	NA	NA	NA	1	2	3	5	5	6	6	7	7	7	8	9	9
WV	NA	NA	NA	NA	NA	NA	NA	NA	NA	3	4	4	5	6	6	6	6	6	5	4	4	3	3
WI	NA	NA	NA	NA	NA	NA	2	3	6	8	9	10	11	11	11	10	10	10	10	9	9	9	8
WY	NA	NA	NA	NA	NA	NA	NA	NA	NA	NA	1	1	1	1	1	1	1	1	1	1	1	1	1
US	65	106	142	186	213	242	232	237	243	293	332	357	391	435	435	435	435	437	435	435	435	435	435

Source: Produced by author.

Notes: Initial seat assignments to states admitted between censuses: After the 1790 census—Kentucky (2, from Virginia); after the 1800 census—Tennessee (1); after the 1810 census—Ohio (1); after the 1820 census—Alabama, Illinois, Indiana, Louisiana, (1 each), Maine (7, from Massachusetts), Mississippi (1); after the 1830 census—none; after the 1840 census—Arkansas, Michigan, (1 each); after the 1850 census—Oregon (1), Minnesota (2); after the 1860 census—Nevada (1), Nebraska (1), West Virginia (3, from Virginia); after the 1870 census—Colorado (1); after the 1880 census—Idaho, Montana, North Dakota, Washington, Wyoming, (1 each), South Dakota (2); after the 1890 census—Utah (1); after the 1900 census—Oklahoma (5); after the 1910 census—Arizona, New Mexico, (1 each); after the 1950 census—Alaska, Hawaii, (1 each).

House Apportionment if Puerto Rico Became a State, 2010

What would the apportionment of the House of Representatives look like if Puerto Rico was to become the 51st state? The most recent population estimates for the states is for July 2009.[2] Using the last four-year 50-state and Puerto Rico population estimates, we can project an estimate of the 2010 state populations and use it to determine an estimate of the apportionment of the 435 House seats.

Caveats

Table 2 is based on the assumption that the apportionment of the House of Representatives is calculated using an estimate of the 2010 population derived from the projected trend line as derived from the 2006 to 2009 state population estimates produced by the U.S. Census Bureau (see footnote 2).The official apportionment based on the 2010 census may differ from this "mock" apportionment based on the projections derived from earlier population estimates for the states.

First, and most importantly, the population of the states will likely grow disproportionately between the time when the earlier estimates were created and the 2010 census period.

Second, population estimates are not directly comparable to actual 2010 census figures. For example, annual population estimates are computed July 1 of the estimate year, whereas the census figures are taken on April 1 of each year ending in zero. Thus, the date used for the estimates differs from that of the 2010 census.

Third, a further complicating factor in using estimates to compute prospective apportionments concerns the status of federal employees who are stationed abroad (chiefly military personnel and their dependents, totaling 574,330 persons in 2000). In 2000, the Census Bureau included this group in the state populations used to reapportion the House.[3] It is expected that the Census Bureau will include this same group in the 2010 apportionment. The estimates used to calculate the prospective apportionment in this report are not adjusted to account for federal employees stationed abroad.

Potential Impact of Puerto Rican Statehood on the 2010 Apportionment

Table 2 shows two comparisons. First, the projected 2010 apportionment of the House of Representatives is shown both without and with Puerto Rico's population included. As can be seen, when Puerto Rico is included as the 51st state, it is allocated six seats in the House of Representatives. Without Puerto Rican statehood, Arizona, Missouri, New York, South Carolina, Texas, and Washington would have been allocated the last six seats rather than Puerto Rico. It is fairly clear that with a population of almost four million people, Puerto Rico's statehood would have an impact on the apportionment process unless the size of the House is increased.

The second comparison, and the more involved, is between the current allocation of seats based on the actual 2000 population and the allocation of the seats based on the projected 2010 population estimates. Examining the "winners" and "losers" with respect to the change between 2000 and 2006, several points are worth noting.

First, Florida, Georgia, Nevada, and Utah would all gain a seat relative to the current allocation, regardless of the status of Puerto Rico.

Second, Arizona would gain two seats relative to its current status, but if Puerto Rico became a state Arizona would only gain one seat. Similarly, Texas would gain four seats relative to its current status, but would only gain three seats if Puerto Rico became a state.

Third, both South Carolina and Washington would gain a seat relative to their current status, but if Puerto Rico became a state, both remain at their 2000 allocation of House seats.

Fourth, California, Illinois, Iowa, Louisiana, Massachusetts, Michigan, Minnesota, New York, and Pennsylvania would all lose a seat relative to the current allocation of House seats, regardless of the status of Puerto Rico. Similarly, Ohio would lose two seats relative to its current allocation, regardless of the status of Puerto Rico.

Fifth, Missouri would lose a seat if Puerto Rico became a state, but would retain the same number of seats relative to its current allocation of House seats if Puerto Rico does not become a state. Similarly, New York would lose two seats if Puerto Rico became a state, but would lose only a single seat relative to its current allocation if Puerto Rico does not become a state.

Table 2. House Apportionment Using Projected 2010 Population Estimates and Including Puerto Rico

State	2010 Projected Population Excluding PR	Projected Seats	2010 Projected Population Including PR	Projected Seats	Projected Gains & Losses due to PR	2000 Apportionment Population	Current Seats	Gains & Losses Relative to 2000 Not Including PR	Gains & Losses Relative to 2000 Including PR
Alabama	4,748,596	7	4,748,596	7	0	4,461,130	7	0	0
Alaska	703,873	1	703,873	1	0	628,933	1	0	0
Arizona	6,749,417	10	6,749,417	9	-1	5,140,683	8	2	1
Arkansas	2,915,784	4	2,915,784	4	0	2,679,733	4	0	0
California	37,262,246	52	37,262,246	52	0	33,930,798	53	-1	-1
Colorado	5,115,833	7	5,115,833	7	0	4,311,882	7	0	0
Connecticut	3,527,173	5	3,527,173	5	0	3,409,535	5	0	0
Delaware	896,717	1	896,717	1	0	785,068	1	0	0
Florida	18,705,656	26	18,705,656	26	0	16,028,890	25	1	1
Georgia	10,013,087	14	10,013,087	14	0	8,206,975	13	1	1
Hawaii	1,301,119	2	1,301,119	2	0	1,216,642	2	0	0
Idaho	1,577,348	2	1,577,348	2	0	1,297,274	2	0	0
Illinois	12,972,881	18	12,972,881	18	0	12,439,042	19	-1	-1

State	2010 Projected Population Excluding PR	Projected Seats	2010 Projected Population Including PR	Projected Seats	Projected Gains & Losses due to PR	2000 Apportionment Population	Current Seats	Gains & Losses Relative to 2000 Not Including PR	Gains & Losses Relative to 2000 Including PR
Indiana	6,466,418	9	6,466,418	9	0	6,090,782	9	0	0
Iowa	3,022,654	4	3,022,654	4	0	2,931,923	5	-1	-1
Kansas	2,839,585	4	2,839,585	4	0	2,693,824	4	0	0
Kentucky	4,348,392	6	4,348,392	6	0	4,049,431	6	0	0
Louisiana	4,597,669	6	4,597,669	6	0	4,480,271	7	-1	-1
Maine	1,320,665	2	1,320,665	2	0	1,277,731	2	0	0
Maryland	5,722,708	8	5,722,708	8	0	5,307,886	8	0	0
Massachusetts	6,632,185	9	6,632,185	9	0	6,355,568	10	-1	-1
Michigan	9,929,751	14	9,929,751	14	0	9,955,829	15	-1	-1
Minnesota	5,307,325	7	5,307,325	7	0	4,925,670	8	-1	-1
Mississippi	2,973,527	4	2,973,527	4	0	2,852,927	4	0	0
Missouri	6,034,962	9	6,034,962	8	-1	5,606,260	9	0	-1
Montana	985,892	1	985,892	1	0	905,316	1	0	0
Nebraska	1,807,376	3	1,807,376	3	0	1,715,369	3	0	0
Nevada	2,704,269	4	2,704,269	4	0	2,002,032	3	1	1

Table 2. (Continued).

State	2010 Projected Population Excluding PR	Projected Seats	2010 Projected Population Including PR	Projected Seats	Projected Gains & Losses due to PR	2000 Apportionment Population	Current Seats	Gains & Losses Relative to 2000 Not Including PR	Gains & Losses Relative to 2000 Including PR
New Hampshire	1,329,564	2	1,329,564	2	0	1,238,415	2	0	0
New Jersey	8,727,578	12	8,727,578	12	0	8,424,354	13	-1	-1
New Mexico	2,031,749	3	2,031,749	3	0	1,823,821	3	0	0
New York	19,597,066	28	19,597,066	27	-1	19,004,973	29	-1	-2
North Carolina	9,570,963	13	9,570,963	13	0	8,067,673	13	0	0
North Dakota	649,169	1	649,169	1	0	643,756	1	0	0
Ohio	11,560,434	16	11,560,434	16	0	11,374,540	18	-2	-2
Oklahoma	3,721,896	5	3,721,896	5	0	3,458,819	5	0	0
Oregon	3,878,380	5	3,878,380	5	0	3,428,543	5	0	0
Pennsylvania	12,652,380	18	12,652,380	18	0	12,300,670	19	-1	-1
Rhode Island	1,049,862	2	1,049,862	2	0	1,049,662	2	0	0
South Carolina	4,643,183	7	4,643,183	6	-1	4,025,061	6	1	0
South Dakota	820,390	1	820,390	1	0	756,874	1	0	0

State	2010 Projected Population Excluding PR	Projected Seats	2010 Projected Population Including PR	Projected Seats	Projected Gains & Losses due to PR	2000 Apportionment Population	Current Seats	Gains & Losses Relative to 2000 Not Including PR	Gains & Losses Relative to 2000 Including PR
Tennessee	6,371,756	9	6,371,756	9	0	5,700,037	9	0	0
Texas	25,249,935	36	25,249,935	35	-1	20,903,994	32	4	3
Utah	2,856,382	4	2,856,382	4	0	2,236,714	3	1	1
Vermont	622,292	1	622,292	1	0	609,890	1	0	0
Virginia	7,956,804	11	7,956,804	11	0	7,100,702	11	0	0
Washington	6,761,110	10	6,761,110	9	-1	5,908,684	9	1	0
West Virginia	1,823,595	3	1,823,595	3	0	1,813,077	3	0	0
Wisconsin	5,682,739	8	5,682,739	8	0	5,371,210	8	0	0
Wyoming	554,340	1	554,340	1	0	495,304	1	0	0
Puerto Rico			3,981,193	6	6				6
TOTALS	309,294,662	435	313,275,855	435		281,424,177	435		

Source: For the 2006-2009 population estimates used in developing the 2010 population projections, see fn. 3, above. For the 2000 population figures and the apportioned seats, see fn. 4, above. State population projections were developed by the author using the FORECAST function in the MS EXCEL spreadsheet package. All apportionment calculations were performed by the author.

INCREASING THE SIZE OF THE HOUSE AND THE TRADITION OF A 435-SEAT HOUSE

The strong 20th century tradition that the total number of Representatives in the House of Representatives should total 435 members might prevent an increase in the House size should Puerto Rico be admitted to statehood.[4]

The U.S. Constitution (Article 1, Section II) requires that "Representatives shall be apportioned among the several states according to their respective numbers, counting the whole number of persons in each state." The requirement that districts must be apportioned *among* states means that district boundaries cannot cross state lines. The Constitution also sets a minimum size for the House of Representatives (one Representative for every state) and a maximum size for the House (one Representative for every 30,000 persons). Congress is free to choose a House size within these parameters by changing the relevant law.

Thus, the House size of 435 may be altered by changing statutory law rather than by enacting a constitutional amendment.[5] Based on the 2010 projection population of 309,294,662 from *Table 2* above, the House could be as large as 10,301 Representatives (based on the constitutional maximum of one Representative for every 30,000 persons). Statehood for Puerto Rico would raise the maximum to 10,443 Members.

The House size was increased in every decade except one in the 19th century to accommodate the growth of the country's population, but the permanent increases stopped after the 1910 census, when the House reached 435 Members. As noted previously, the House size was increased temporarily to 437 in 1960, to accommodate the admission of Alaska and Hawaii as states, but the total went back to 435 in 1963, with the new reapportionment following the 1960 census.

Although one cannot say for sure why the House size has not been permanently increased since the 1910 census, the arguments most often raised center on efficiency and cost. Proponents of the status quo suggest that a larger House would work less efficiently and at greater cost, due to Member and staff salaries and allowances. Proponents of increasing the House size often argue that other legislative bodies seem to work well with larger memberships, and less populous districts might give minorities greater representation in Congress. Since 1940, the average population of a congressional district has more than doubled (from 303,827 in 1940 to 646,946 in 2000).

End Notes

[1] For a general discussion of the history of admitting states to the union, see CRS Report 98-702 GOV, *Statehood Process of the Fifty States*, by Garrine P. Laney (out-of-print report, available from the author upon request).

[2] U.S. Department of Commerce, U.S. Census Bureau, "Texas Gains the Most in Population, Last State Population Estimates Before 2010 Census Count," press release, December 23, 2009, see detailed tables, Annual Population Estimates 2000 to 2009, available at the Census Bureau's website, http://www.census.gov/popest/states

[3] CRS Report RS20768, *House Apportionment 2000: States Gaining, Losing, and on the Margin*, by Royce Crocker, p. 3. This report also describes how the equal proportions formula allocates Representatives among the states.

[4] If Puerto Rico was to be admitted to statehood with a proviso that the Census Bureau first calculate how many seats it would have been entitled to under a 435-seat House, and then add that total to the House size for the final calculation (resulting in 441 seats), Puerto Rico would still obtain six seats; the six states that otherwise would each have lost a seat with a 435-seat House would thus have retained the seats. (The fact that the same six states would regain the seats that they lost to Puerto Rico in the above scenarios would not necessarily hold in all such scenarios. It is possible that increasing the House size could change the states' fractional shares allocated by the apportionment formula so that not all the "losing states" would necessarily regain the lost seats; other states might have greater claims. For a more complete discussion of how the apportionment formula works, please see CRS Report RL31074, *The House of Representatives Apportionment Formula: An Analysis of Proposals for Change and Their Impact on States*, by Royce Crocker.)

[5] 46 Stat. 21, 26-27, as codified in 2 U.S.C. 2a(a).

The House of Representatives... ISBN: 978-1-61324-308-4
Editors: R. D. Orsino, O. G. Trance

Chapter 12

STRENGTH IN NUMBERS: YOUR GUIDE TO CENSUS 2010 REDISTRICTING DATA FROM THE U.S. CENSUS BUREAU

Once every 10 years, Americans stand up to be counted. Downtown and out-of-town, in the mountains and on the farms, we speak up and let our governments know that we intend to be represented in the decisions that they make.

The census gives us an opportunity to be part of the democratic process. Census numbers ensure that our representative districts—for the U.S. Congress and for state legislatures, and in our city and town governments—reflect our numbers, north or south, east or west.

This brochure explains where census numbers come from and the role those numbers have in the way states and localities redraw the boundaries of their legislative districts. The information here looks in particular at the maps and numbers that state governments and others get from the Census Bureau and use in redistricting.

WHY A CENSUS?

The U.S. Census Bureau, part of the U.S. Department of Commerce, conducts the decennial census and issues population numbers. But the federal government conducted a census long before the Census Bureau was created in 1902.

The first census was taken in 1790. Article 1, Section 2, of the U.S. Constitution established that the apportionment of the U.S. House of Representatives shall be based upon a national census. The census has many other important uses. It affects our lives in ways we don't often realize. The road you take to work each day, the hospital that serves your community, the schools your children attend, the products your grocery stocks—all these have been influenced by the census.

Governments use census statistics, for example, in planning needed highways or in locating new services or schools. Businesses use census numbers in marketing new products and locating new stores.

The imagination is the only limit upon the uses of the statistics that come out of the census.

THE CENSUS AT A GLANCE

In early March 2010, the U.S. Postal Service delivered a letter to households announcing that the 2010 Census would be coming and alerting everyone to watch for the census form. The 2010 Census questionnaire arrived shortly thereafter, and the Census Bureau asked all households to return the forms using April 1, 2010, as the reference date. Some households in hard-to-count areas received the initial questionnaire and then redeliveries of the questionnaire. The Census Bureau used enumerators to take the census in rural areas and check on questionnaires that had not been returned by mail.

The questionnaires were sent to one of three processing offices, where digital scanners read the unique barcode on each questionnaire through the envelope window to record its return status. The questionnaires were optically scanned and converted to digital images. All information was further processed and tabulated at the Census Bureau's secure computer center in Bowie, Maryland.

Finally, the Census Bureau generates the geographic and summary file data for you to use in redistricting. Media to bring you the data will include DVD-ROMs and the American FactFinder, which is the Census Bureau's data access and dissemination system on the Internet at <www.census.gov>.

CONFIDENTIALITY IS A MUST

Title 13 of the U.S. Code contains the laws governing the Census Bureau. Section 9 of Title 13 assures the confidentiality of information gathered by the Census Bureau. It specifies that neither the Secretary of C ommerce nor any other officer or employee of the Department of Commerce—in fact, no one—may use the information furnished under the provisions of this title for any purpose other than the statistical purposes for which the information is supplied.

The law also states that no Census Bureau tabulation can identify any particular establishment or individual and that no one other than the sworn officers and employees of the Census Bureau can examine information supplied in response to censuses and surveys. Only after 72 years are the census schedules opened to public inspection and use.

Redistricting Must Aim at Equality

The decennial census has played a crucial role in the apportionment of the Congress for more than two centuries. But it is only in the last 35 years that the Census Bureau has played a major role in the redistricting process.

U.S. Supreme Court decisions handed down during the 1960s clarified the Constitution's intention to provide equality of representation for all Americans. In 1964, the *Wesberry v. Sanders* decision held that, "as nearly as is practicable one person's vote in a congressional election is to be worth as much as another's." That same year, in *Reynolds v. Sims*, the Court ruled that state legislative districts must be "as nearly of equal population as is practicable."

Both U.S. congressional districts and state legislative districts must be drawn so that their residents have a fair and equal share in the way they are governed. These Supreme Court decisions increased the states' need for geographically detailed census information in the redistricting process.

The urgency of the states' need for these data led the Congress to pass Public Law (P.L.) 94-171 in December 1975.

Taking the Census

Before we look at the statistics, maps, and electronic geographic files that states will use in redistricting, let's look at the census itself—the undertaking through which the Census Bureau gathers the statistics and the important first step in the redistricting process.

The Census Bureau began to prepare for the twenty-third decennial census long before 2010. For the public, however, the process began in March 2010 when census questionnaires were mailed to most households in the United States. In some rural areas, census takers delivered questionnaires. People filled out the questionnaire using a reference date of April 1, 2010—Ce nsus Day—and returned them by mail. In some instances, a census taker visited a household to collect the census information.

To conduct the census, the Census Bureau hires enumerators working out of 494 local census offices nationwide. To process the questionnaires, we use three data capture centers. People living in populous areas mail their forms directly to a data capture center. In less populous areas, census staff leave a questionnaire at each household for a resident to fill out and mail back in a postage-paid envelope or staff will perform an in-person interview. In all cases, if a form is not received, the Census Bureau attempts to follow up with a personal visit to try to collect the information. The data capture centers are located in Baltimore, Maryland; Jeffersonville, Indiana; and Phoenix, Arizona.

As soon as a form reaches a data capture center, the clock starts ticking for the Census Bureau. These centers use scanners to record the arrival of the questionnaires, so we can keep an automated list of forms returned and those still outstanding.

The data capture centers use optical scanners to capture a picture of each questionnaire form and extract the data. Once the Census Bureau has completed the processing of the census forms, we begin to compile final data in the our Washington offices. Census Day, April 1, 2010, may be the most conspicuous date on our calendar, but it's not our only one. Now we face several deadlines in processing the final census counts.

The Department of Commerce and the Census Bureau provide census counts to the President and the states by the deadlines set forth in Title 13 of the U.S. Code (U.S.C.) Section 141 (b) and (c). For the 2010 Census, the Secretary of Commerce and the Census Bureau Director will report the total population counts by state to the President by December 31, 2010. By April 1, 2011, the Director will provide the detailed population counts for all areas within each state to the governors and legislative leaders, under the provisions of Public Law 94-171.

U.S. Census Bureau
Dr. Robert M. Groves, Director
Thomas L. Mesenbourg, Jr., Deputy Director
Census 2010 Redistricting Data Office
Cathy C. McCully, Chief
James Whitehorne, Assistant Chief

2010 Census Leadership

Dr. Robert M. Groves,
Director
the Decennial Census

Thomas L. Mesenbourg,
Deputy Director

Arnold Jackson,
Associate Director for
the Decennial Census

Robert M. Groves is the Director of the U.S. Census Bureau

President Barack Obama nominated Robert M. Groves for director of the U.S. Census Bureau on April 2, 2009, and the Senate confirmed him on July 13, 2009. He began his tenure as director on July 15, 2009. Groves had been a professor at the University of Michigan and director of its Survey Research Center, as well as research professor at the Joint Program in Survey Methodology at the University of Maryland. He was the Census Bureau's Associate Director for Statistical Design, Methodology and Standards from 1990 to 1992, on loan from the University of Michigan.

Thomas L. Mesenbourg is the Deputy Director of the U.S. Census Bureau Since May 2, 2008, Mesenbourg has been serving as Deputy Director and Chief Operating Officer, overseeing the day-to-day operations of the government's preeminent statistical agency. The Bureau has about 12,000 employees - nearly 5,000 at Suitland, Md., headquarters and the rest are based at regional offices and telephone centers across the country.

Arnold Jackson is the Associate Director for Decennial Census at the U.S. Census Bureau.

He provides executive leadership for all decennial census and related programs, and is principal adviser to the executive staff, providing overall direction, planning and coordination for all decennial census operations. He works closely with the six decennial division chiefs and two program office chiefs to provide overall direction for reengineering the 2010 Census.

APPORTIONMENT *IS THE* FUNDAMENTAL USE

According to the Constitution, the census has one fundamental purpose: to ensure that the representation of each state in the U.S. House of Representatives reflects the relative size of its population as compared with other states.

There are 435 representatives divided up among the 50 states. Each one of these representatives is elected by the voters of a congressional district.

Populous states have more representatives than less populous states. In the 111th Congress, California had 53 representatives. Wyoming, the least populous state, had just one. The map on this page shows how many representatives each state had as a result of Census 2000.

"Apportionment" is the process of determining how many representatives each state is entitled to. How does the Census Bureau figure in this process? Our role is twofold—to conduct the census and, as a part of the Executive Branch, to calculate the apportionment based upon the census results. Once we take the census and compile the results, we then use the method of equal proportions to determine the number of representatives each state receives. But our job doesn't end there.

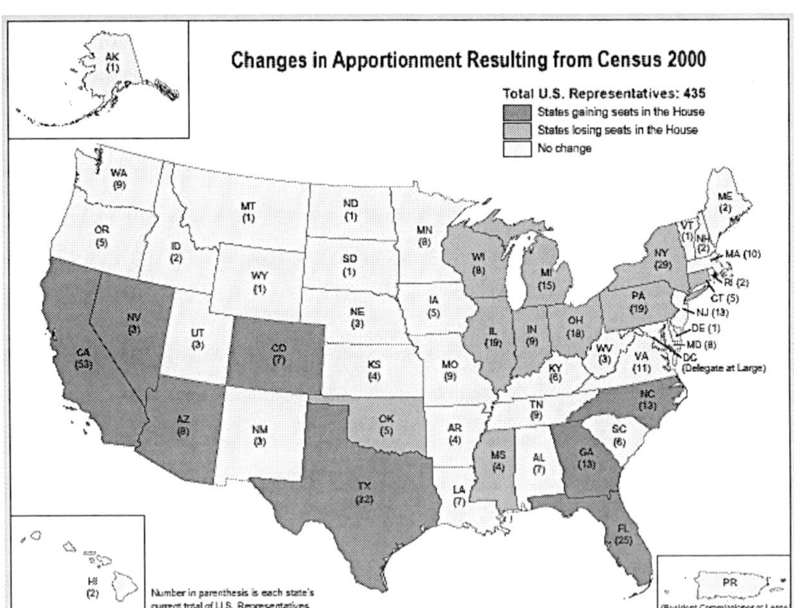

In 2000, the South and West Gained Seats!

"One person/one vote" court decisions and legislation have given the Census Bureau a major role in redistricting, the process by which state governments redraw U.S. congressional and state legislative districts.

Off to the President

The Census Bureau must prepare the final, offcial state population counts required for the apportionment of the U.S. House of Representatives.

These offcial counts are to be reported to the President on or before December 31, 2010, a brief 9 months after Census Day. According to the U.S. Code, the President must then report these figures to the Congress. He will do this in early January 2011, during the first week of the 112th Congress. This report will show:

- The population of each state.
- The number of representatives apportioned to each state.

The apportionment section of the U.S. Code also tells the steps that are to be followed after the Congress receives the President's report. Within 15 calendar days, the Clerk of the House of Representatives must send to each state's governor a certificate showing how many representatives the state may send to the next Congress.

With this information and with the data provided by the U.S. Census Bureau, the states and nongovernmental organizations—in fact anyone with access to geographic information system software—will have the ability to design district boundaries using desktop computers, laptop computers, or the Internet.

Method of Equal Proportions Guides Apportionment

How does the method of equal proportions work?

Adopted in 1941 (U.S. Code, Title 2, Section 2a), the method of equal proportions requires the Census Bureau to compile a priority list of states. Priority value is determined by dividing a state's population by the geometric mean of its current and next House seats.

For example, following Census 2000, each of the 50 states was awarded 1 seat out of the current 435 total. Then, the fifty-first seat went to the state that had the highest priority value for its second seat.

In computing the apportionment from the 2000 state totals, seat 51 went to California, whose priority value under the method of equal proportions was 23,992,697. The next seat, number 52, went to Texas, with a second-seat priority value of 14,781,356; California received seat number 53, with a priority value of 13,852,190; and New York received seat number 54, with a priority value of 13,438,545.

Once the number of seats assigned to the individual states is determined, the task of drawing the new congressional districts is generally that of each state legislature.

For Census 2000 values, see <www.census.gov/population/www/censusdata/apportionment/files/00pvalues .txt>.

For additional details on computing apportionment, see <www.census.gov /population/www/censusdata / apportionment/computing.html>.

The Redistricting Process Begins

But wait! The clock is still ticking! The Census Bureau still has another important deadline to meet.

In December 1975, the Congress passed Public Law (P.L.) 94-171. This law requires the Census Bureau to make special preparations to provide redistricting data to the 50 states no later than April 1 of the year following a census (so April 1, 2011, for the 2010 Census). P.L. 94-171 specifies that within 1 year of Census Day, the Census Bureau must send each state the small-area data the state will need to redraw districts for the state legislature.

P.L. 94-171 sets up a voluntary program between the Census Bureau and those states that wish to receive population tabulations for voting districts and other state-specified geographic areas.

Under this program, those responsible for the legislative apportionment or redistricting of each state may devise a plan identifying the voting districts for which they want the specific tabulations and submit it to the Census Bureau.

Beginning in 2005, the Redistricting Data Office of the Census Bureau met with state officials in 46 states. These meetings explained the timeline and programs available for the 2010 Census, providing states the time to prepare and allocate resources in advance of the census. The states also provided the Census Bureau with valuable feedback on census program planning.

The 2010 Census Redistricting Data Program is a five-phase program. During Phase 1 (2005–2006), the Census Bureau collected state legislative district boundaries and associated updates to tabulate legislative districts. This phase also included an aggressive 2010 Census communications plan, with visits to state capitals, to make sure the states were informed and prepared for the upcoming census.

Phase 2 (2008–2010) consisted of the Voting District/Block Boundary Suggestion Project (VTD/BBSP) in which states received TIGER/ Line® shapefiles and the MAF/TIGER Partnership Software (MTPS) to electronically collect voting district boundaries, feature updates, suggested block boundaries, and corrected state legislative district boundaries. Both Phase 1 and Phase 2 are voluntary programs that include a step where the state verifies the submitted data.

Phase 3 constitutes the delivery of the data for the 2010 Census. The Census Bureau will deliver the geographic and data products to the majority and minority leadership in the state legislatures, the governors, and any designated P.L. 94-171 liaisons. Once bipartisan receipt of the data is confirmed, the data will be made available online to the public within 24 hours through the American FactFinder. For this census, the P.L. 94-171 data will include population counts for small areas within each state, as well as housing occupied/vacancy counts.

After the Census Bureau provides the data, the states will begin their redistricting. States are responsible for delineating their own congressional and legislative boundaries and their legislatures. Legislatures, secretaries of state, governors, and/or redistricting commissions carry out the process.

During Phase 4 (2011–2013) the Census Bureau's Redistricting Data Offce will collect the post-2010 Census state legislative and congressional district plans. We will retabulate the 2010 redistricting data for the 113th Congress and newly drawn state legislative districts. The American Community Survey (ACS) will also present data for these new areas. (See below for more information on the ACS.)

The final phase of the 2010 Census Redistricting Data Program, Phase 5, will be an evaluation and solicitation of recommendations for the 2020 Census. Working with the National Conference of State Legislatures, the Census Bureau will conduct a historical review by the states of the successes and failures of the Census Bureau to meet the P.L. 94-171 mandate. These findings will be used to develop recommendations for the 2020 Census Redistricting Data Program.

Cathy McCully, chief, and James Whitehorne, assistant chief, Redistricting Data Office are responsible for ensuring all phases of the redistricting data program are managed successfully, including the delivery of the P.L. 94-171 data by April 1, 2011.

Census 2010 Redistricting Data Program					
Phase 1 and Phase 2 Participation (SLDU/SLDL and VTD/BBSP)					
	VTD	BBS	SLDU	SLD	CD
Alabama	x		x	x	x
Alaska	x	x	x	x	AL
Arizona	x	x	x	x	x
Arkansas	x		x	x	x
California	x	x	x	x	x
Colorado	x	x	x	x	x
Connecticut	x		x	x	x
Delaware	x		x	x	AL
District Of Columbia	x		x	##	NV

Census 2010 Redistricting Data Program					
Phase 1 and Phase 2 Participation (SLDU/SLDL and VTD/BBSP)					
Florida	x	x	x	x	x
Georgia	x	x	x	x	x
Hawaii	x	x	x	x	x
Idaho	x		x	x	x
Illinois	x	x	x	x	x
Indiana	x	x	x	x	x
Iowa	x		x	x	x
Kansas	x		x	x	x
Kentucky			x	x	x
Louisiana	x	x	x	x	x
Maine	x		x	x	x
Maryland	x	x	x	x	x
Massachusetts	x		x	x	x
Michigan	x	x	x	x	x
Minnesota	x	x	x	x	x
Mississippi	x		x	x	x
Missouri	x		x	x	x
Montana	x (see		x	x	AL
Nebraska	x	x	x	##	x
Nevada	x		x	x	x
New Hampshire	x		x	x	x
New Jersey	x		x	x	x
New Mexico	x	x	x	x	x
New York	x		x	x	x
North Carolina	x		x	x	x
North Dakota	x		x	x	AL
Ohio	x		x	x	x
Oklahoma	x	x	x	x	x
Oregon	x (see	x	x	x	x
Pennsylvania	x		x	x	x
Rhode Island	Did not participate for Phase 2				

(Continued).

Census 2010 Redistricting Data Program					
Phase 1 and Phase 2 Participation (SLDU/SLDL and VTD/BBSP)					
South Carolina	x	x	x	x	x
South Dakota	x		x	x	AL
Tennessee	x	x	x	x	x
Texas	x		x	x	x
Utah	x	x	x	x	x
Vermont	x		x	x	AL
Virginia	x		x	x	x
Washington	x	x	x	x	x
West Virginia	x		x	x	x
Wisconsin	x		x	x	x
Wyoming	x		x	x	AL
Puerto Rico	x		x	x	NV

Montana: the following counties submitted VTDs for Phase 2: 001, 005, 007, 009, 011, 013, 017, 019, 023, 025, 029, 031, 033, 035, 037, 043, 049, 051, 059, 063, 065, 067, 069, 073, 075, 079, 081, 085, 089, 091, 093, 095, 103,105, 109, 111

Oregon: only county 051 submitted VTDs for Phase 2.

State Legislative Districts: Original SLDs were collected during Phase 1 of the RDP. Delaware, South Dakota, Indiana, and Utah submitted new plans in 2008.

All states contain complete coverage for SLDUs.

- The District of Columbia has city council wards. Nebraska's legislature is unicameral. Therefore, these two state/state equivalents have no SLDL coverage.

Congressional Districts: These were last collected for the 110th Congress, and there were no changes for the 111th Congressional Districts for Census 2010.

AL - At Large Congressional Representation NV - Non-Voting Congressional Delegation

BBSP - Block Boundary Suggestions

CD - Congressional District

RDP - Redistricting Data Program

SLDL - State Legislative District Lower (House) SLDU - State Legislative District Upper (Senate) VTD - Voting District

MAF/TIGER Partnership Software

Advances in geographic information system (GIS) software and the wide adoption of the use of digital geographic data meant that the 2010 Redistricting Data Program (RDP) could be conducted solely as a digital exchange. During the years before the 2010 Census, the Census Bureau, through a contractor, developed a customized GIS to help states update census-provided geographic data and return the updates to the Census Bureau for inclusion in the MAF/TIGER database. From this, the MAF/TIGER Partnership Software (MTPS) was created. All RDP participants received the MTPS, along with a full suite of data files for their state. The MTPS allowed participants to add linear features, create or update their redistricting entity boundaries, apply block boundary suggestions, and update areal water bodies and area landmarks. In addition, participants could bring in their own geographic data or imagery as a reference tool for making their changes. The MTPS featured data-quality tools to help identify and eliminate some commonly occurring data errors. Once participants completed their work, the MTPS packaged all of the updated information into a single compressed file that could be sent by file transfer protocol (FTP) to the Census Bureau for processing.

Out Goes the Long Form and in Comes the American Community Survey

Designed to replace the long form used in past decennial censuses, the American Community Survey (ACS) is conducted by the Census Bureau in every county, American Indian and Alaska Native Area, and Hawaiian Home Land. It began in 1996 in a sample of counties across the country. Today the survey is conducted in 250,000 households per month throughout all U.S. counties and in all municipios in Puerto Rico, where it is called the Puerto Rico Community Survey.

While the 2010 Census focuses on counting the population for purposes of apportionment and redistricting, the ACS provides yearly data similar to that available from the long form used in previous decennial censuses. The questions cover such topics as journey to work; age; income and housing; race, Hispanic origin, and language spoken at home; military service; and more. While most redistricting plans are based on the P.L. 94-171 data and other statewide data, the ACS also will be of interest to those drawing plans since plans are routinely analyzed. Experts will analyze demographic characteristics such as citizenship and language ability when reviewing congressional and legislative plans. ACS estimates are released annually as 1-year, 3-year and 5-year estimates based on population thresholds. The 5-year estimates provide ACS data at the nationwide level down to small geographic areas such as state legislative district, census tract, and block group. Many redistricting experts will use 5-year ACS estimates when they review redistricting plans.

Tools To Do the Job

When state offcials begin the diffcult task of redrawing their districts, they'll have in hand several important tools resulting from census redistricting data:

- 2010 Census Redistricting Data [P.L. 94-171] Summary Files
- 2010 Census P.L. 94-171 Voting District/State Legislative District Reference Maps
- 2010 Census P.L. 94-171 County Block Maps
- 2010 Census Tract Reference Maps
- 2010 Census School District Reference Maps
- 2010 Census Tabulation Geography TIGER/Line® Shapefiles

- 2010 Census Tabulation Geography Block Assignment Files for Congressional Districts, State Legislative District Upper Chambers, State Legislative District Lower Chambers, Voting Districts, Elementary School Districts, Secondary School Districts, and Unified School Districts

The P.L. 94-171 summaries have population totals and summaries by race, Hispanic or Latino, and voting age for all appropriate geographic areas delimited on the maps: state, counties or equivalent areas, state legislative districts, voting districts, county subdivisions, school districts, places, American Indian/Alaska Native/Native Hawaiian areas, census tracts, block groups, and blocks.

New for the 2010 Census, housing unit counts will be included as part of the 2010 Census Redistricting Data [P.L. 94-171] Summary Files. Also for 2010, states recommended including school districts as part of the geographic summary levels and a new table on housing unit occupancy status.

Public Law 94-171 Tabulations

While P.L. 94-171 requires the Census Bureau to furnish only counts of the total population, additional data items are included. Since the inception of the Census Redistricting Data Program for the 1980 census, the Census Bureau has included summaries for the major race groups specified by the Statistical Programs and Standards Offce of the U.S. Offce of Management and Budget (OMB) in Directive 15 (as issued in 1977 and revised in 1997).

Originally the tabulation groups included White, Black, American Indian/Alaska Native, and Asian/Pacific Islander, plus "some other race." These race data were also cross-tabulated by Hispanic/Non-Hispanic origin.

At the request of the state legislatures and the Department of Justice, for the 1990 Census Redistricting Data Program, voting age (18 years old and over) was added to the cross-tabulation of race and Hispanic origin.

Census Statistics for 2010: The American FactFinder

The American FactFinder (AFF) is a data-access system that gives users facts and information about communities, the economy, and society. The interactive electronic system allows data users access to pre defined data products, metadata, and online help, as well as the ability to create custom data products online. This dissemination method allows for a quicker release of the detailed data users want. Users may access data and create their own reports. The AFF currently offers data from the 2000 decennial census, the American Community Survey, the Population Estimates Program, and the 2002 and 2007 economic censuses, and annual economic surveys. It also will provide data from the 2010 Census. The 2010 Census Redistricting Data [P.L. 94-171] Summary File will be available, by state, through the AFF within 24 hours after the bipartisan acknowledgement of its receipt by each state's designated officials.

The volumes of data collected by the Census Bureau require a large and efficient system of dissemination. With AFF, Census Bureau customers have more flexibility to request the data they need for their geography of interest. The AFF provides for a quick release of detailed data about the nation's people and the economy to meet the needs of data users. To access the American Fact-Finder, go to the Census Bureau home page at <www.census.gov>.

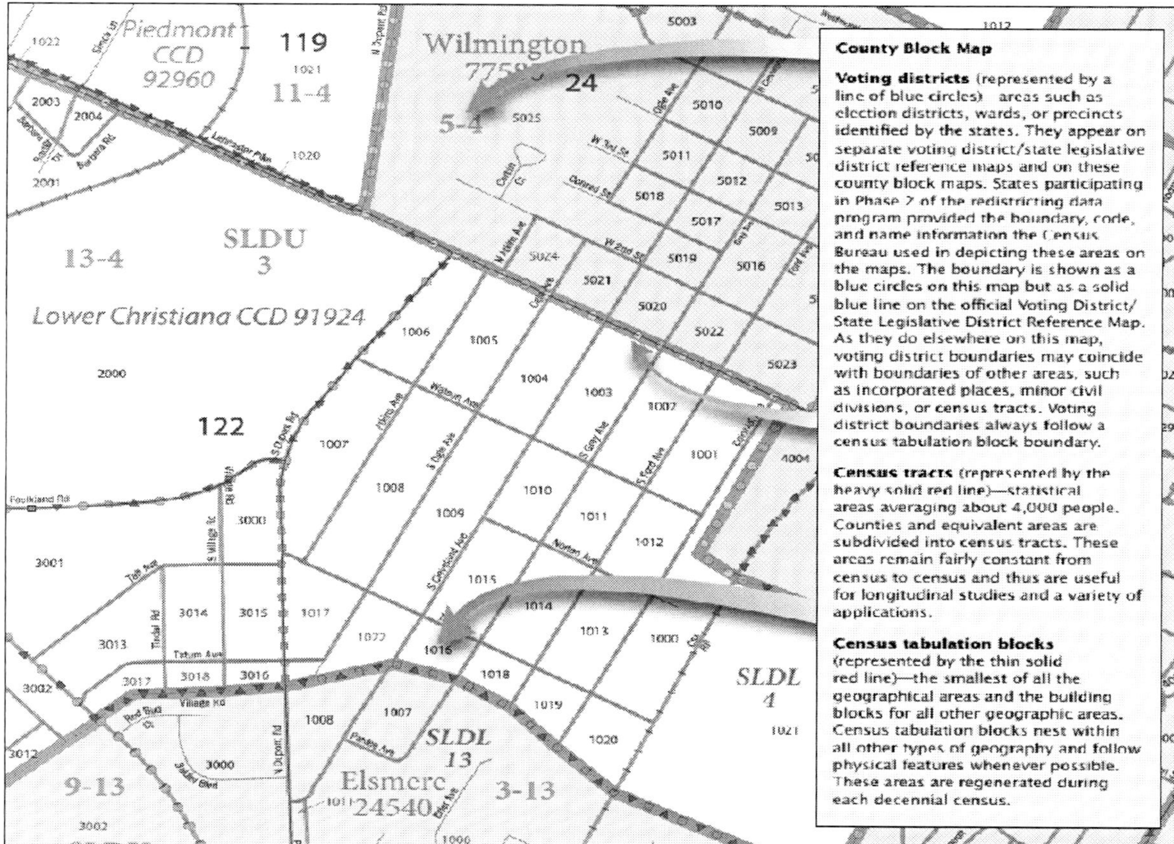
County Block Map
Voting districts (represented by a line of blue circles) areas such as election districts, wards, or precincts identified by the states. They appear on separate voting district/state legislative district reference maps and on these county block maps. States participating in Phase 2 of the redistricting data program provided the boundary, code, and name information the Census Bureau used in depicting these areas on the maps. The boundary is shown as a blue circles on this map but as a solid blue line on the official Voting District/ State Legislative District Reference Map. As they do elsewhere on this map, voting district boundaries may coincide with boundaries of other areas, such as incorporated places, minor civil divisions, or census tracts. Voting district boundaries always follow a census tabulation block boundary.
Census tracts (represented by the heavy solid red line)—statistical areas averaging about 4,000 people. Counties and equivalent areas are subdivided into census tracts. These areas remain fairly constant from census to census and thus are useful for longitudinal studies and a variety of applications.
Census tabulation blocks (represented by the thin solid red line)—the smallest of all the geographical areas and the building blocks for all other geographic areas. Census tabulation blocks nest within all other types of geography and follow physical features whenever possible. These areas are regenerated during each decennial census.
Piedmont CCD 92960
119
11-4
Wilmington
24
5-4
SLDU 3
13-4
Lower Christiana CCD 91924
122
SLDL 4
SLDL 13
Elsmere 24540
3-13
9-13

You Need to Map Things Out!

The data presented in the P.L. 94-171 data set won't mean much until you look at the supporting geographic products and learn a little about the geographic areas. The Census Bureau has made the Census 2010 maps as clear as we can to convey the greatest detail about small areas. The maps are on as few map sheets as possible, are digital, and are in portable document format (.pdf). The scale varies from county to county depending on area size and population density, and in many areas insets are used to ensure a readable map. We made the maps using our TIGER® system, an automated geographic database the Census Bureau first developed for the 1990 census and updates and maintains to support all Census Bureau censuses and surveys, including the 2010 Census.

This system provides the ability to develop nationwide block-level data that legislatures request. Data users easily can review the .pdf maps or data without ever unfolding a map sheet! Voting district/state legislative district reference maps (see example, page 7) cover a county or equivalent area and show the outline of voting districts (if defined) and state legislative districts. These maps provide a quick picture of areas that can be used as references for constructing new legislative districts. These maps also show the boundaries of the current state legislative districts.

When greater detail is needed, county block maps (page 6) are the reference to consult. These maps show the smallest tabulation areas—census blocks—that can be used in the redistricting process. Map sheets are organized by county. For the block map, an index sheet shows the layout of the relationship between individual map sheets within the county.

TIGER/Line® Shapefiles

Think of the TIGER (Topologically Integrated Geographic Encoding and Referencing system) database, as provided in our TIGER/Line® shapefile products, as a huge map of the United States. That's basically what it is. It includes geographic data for visible features on the earth's surface—features such as roads, railroads, and streams. For most features, the TIGER/Line® shapefiles also include attributes, such as the names of the feature, and for streets, the potential address range and associated ZIP Code for each side of the street. The TIGER/Line® shapefiles also include the boundaries and codes for all geographic areas for which the Census Bureau tabulates data, including

American Indian/Alaska Native areas, states, counties, townships, cities, and similar functioning general-purpose governments. It also has the boundaries and codes for statistical areas (such as census tracts and census blocks) for which the Census Bureau collects and tabulates data.

The Census Bureau developed the TIGER system jointly with the U.S. Geological Survey (USGS) in the 1980s. We combined detailed USGS digital data (based on map sheets in which 1 inch equals approximately 1.6 miles) with digital data from the geographic base files used in the 1980 census. We continue to update the TIGER database (streets, address ranges, and political boundaries) based on information we obtain from local and tribal governments, the U.S. Postal Service, and our own field staff.

In the 2000s, we undertook a major realignment of the TIGER database, through the MAF/TIGER Accuracy Improvement Project, using imagery to improve its spatial accuracy. By the time we finished in 2007, TIGER had an accuracy of 7.6 meters or better.

Just before we tabulate the 2010 Census data, we will use the TIGER database to assign the census tabulation block numbers for all census blocks in the entire nation, using the updated base features and geographic area boundaries. This will best ensure that Census 2010 tabulation blocks are meaningful and represent the latest possible information.

Because the TIGER database contains legal and statistical geographic areas and codes, and the underlying street network, users now have a powerful tool to display demographic data graphically. Using the TIGER/Line® shapefiles (the public version of the TIGER database) and appropriate software, you can rapidly determine the impact on the demographic makeup of a district when you move a boundary. You can quickly perform this analysis at all levels, from city blocks to congressional districts.

TIGER/Line® shapefiles will be available with all of the 2010 Census geographic codes shortly before the 2010 Census summary file data become available. All of the 2009 TIGER/Line® shapefiles for the nation comprise approximately 55 gigabytes of compressed data or 92 gigabytes of uncompressed data. The smallest state or state equivalent is about 32 kilobytes uncompressed, while the largest is over 6.7 gigabytes uncompressed. The 2010 TIGER/Line® shapefiles will be in similar size ranges.

Voting districts—areas such as election districts, wards, or precincts identified by the states. They appear on separate voting district/state legislative district reference maps and on the county block maps.

States participating in the redistricting data program provided the boundary, code, and name information we used in depicting these areas on the maps. The boundary is shown as a shaded stippled pattern on this map but may be different on the offcial 2010 Census maps. As they do elsewhere on this map, voting district boundaries may coincide with boundaries of other areas, such an incorporated places, minor civil divisions, or census tracts, and they always follow a census block boundary.

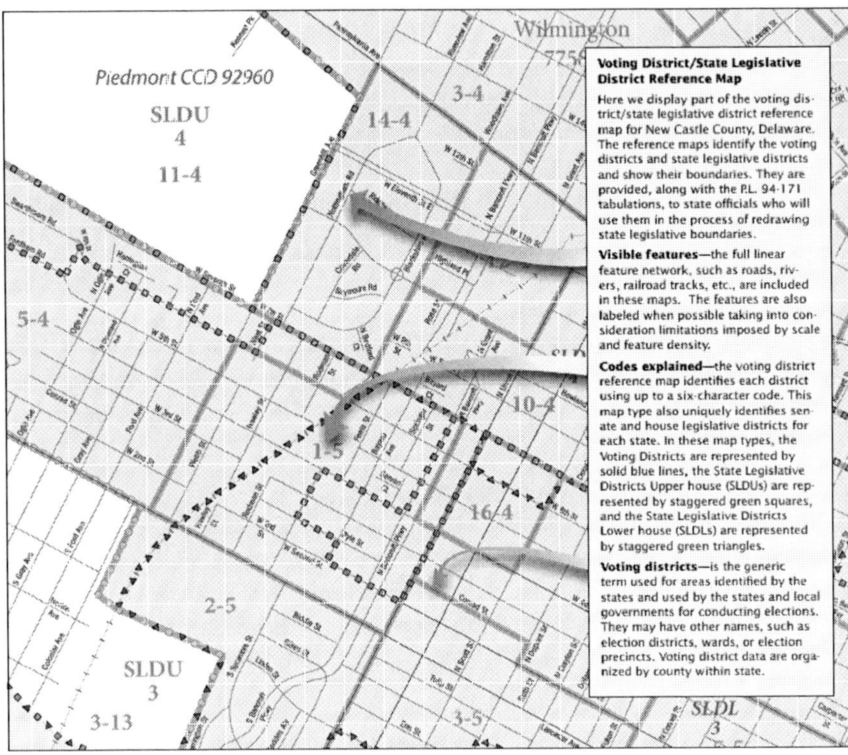

Census tracts—statistical areas averaging about 4,000 people. Counties and equivalent areas are subdivided into census tracts. These areas remain fairly constant from census to census and thus are useful for longitudinal studies and a variety of applications.

Legislative districts—districts used to elect a member to the upper (senate) or lower (house) chambers of state legislatures. As with voting districts, states could define these at their option. Please see the chart on page 4 for further information on how states participated in the definition of voting districts and legislative districts.

Census tabulation blocks—smallest of census geographic areas, normally bounded by streets or other prominent physical features or by the boundaries of geographic areas. They may be as small as a typical city block that's bounded by four streets or larger than 100 square miles in some rural areas. Blocks are identified by a four-digit number, unique within census tracts for the 2010 Census.

Nationally, blocks average about 100 people each. Block groups—a set of census blocks identified by the same first digit within a census tract. For example, all blocks in a census tract in the 1000 range define block group 1.

Once you study the map series and definitions shown here, you'll be ready to work with the statistics for these areas.

Record Layout for P.L. 94-171 Data

Earlier we mentioned that the Census Bureau will furnish each governor and the majority and minority leaders of each state legislature with a full set of their state's census redistricting data. The law requires us to do this by April 1, 2011.

While P.L. 94-171 requires the Census Bureau to furnish only counts of the total population, additional data also will be included. Cathy McCully, chief of the Census 2010 Redistricting Data Offce, notes, "We'll provide data on the voting-age population and cross-tabulations of voting age by race characteristics, as well as by Hispanic or Latino." For the 2010 Census, the Census Bureau carried out extensive consultations between 2005 and 2009 with stakeholders in the redistricting process.

During this period, the Census Bureau conducted the 2010 Census Dress Rehearsal in April 2008 in the city of San Joaquin, California. In keeping with the criteria from the 2010 Census, each of the "single race" categories (5 plus "some other race"), plus the 57 possible categories for those who choose more than one race were included. This approach produced up to 63 racial tallies and will provide users the maximum flexibility for analyzing these new data for any area. This flexible design also meets the needs of the Department of Justice for enforcement of civil rights programs.

During the evaluation phase of the program, states will make recommendations for the next census. James Whitehorne, assistant chief of the 2010 Census Redistricting Data Offce notes, "We are including a housing unit table on vacancy status in the 2010 P.L. summary levels. This recommendation is similar to the inclusion of housing units during the 1990 Census."

At each step of the process for collecting and tabulating these P.L.94-171 redistricting data, the Census Bureau will take the necessary steps to protect the confidentiality of individual responses.

Hispanic/Latino origin is not considered a race category. Race and Hispanic/Latino data are obtained from a separate question on the 2010 Census questionnaire. The chart starting on page 9 shows a portion of the computer record layout for how these data will be arrayed on DVD, along with the geography that will link the P.L. redistricting data to each block, voting district, census tract, city, county, etc.

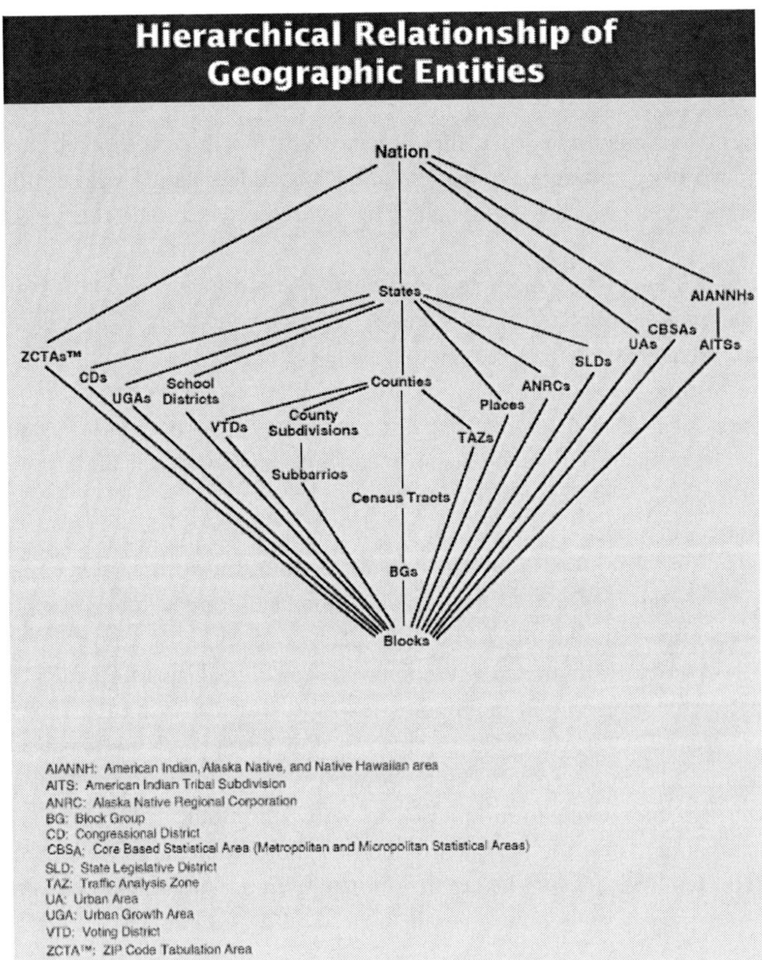

2010 Census Redistricting Data (Public Law 94-171)
Summary File - EXTRACT
SUMMARY TABLE OUTLINES Final v2.0

Table No.	Cell Count	Indent	
P1.		0	RACE [71]
P1.		0	Universe: Total population
P1.	1	0	Total:
P1.	2	1	Population of one race:
P1.	3	2	White alone
P1.	4	2	Black or African American alone
P1.	5	2	American Indian and Alaska Native alone
P1.	6	2	Asian alone
P1.	7	2	Native Hawaiian and Other Pacific Islander alone
P1.	8	2	Some Other Race alone
P1.	9	1	Two or More Races:
P1.	10	2	Population of two races:
P1.	11	3	White; Black or African American
P1.	12	3	White; American Indian and Alaska Native
P1.	13	3	White; Asian
P1.	14	3	White; Native Hawaiian and Other Pacific Islander
P1.	15	3	White; Some Other Race
P1.	16	3	Black or African American; American Indian and Alaska Native

(Continued).

Table No.	Cell Count	Indent				
P1.	17	3				Black or African American; Asian
P1.	18	3				Black or African American; Native Hawaiian and Other Pacific Islander
P1.	19	3				Black or African American; Some Other Race
P1.	20	3				American Indian and Alaska Native; Asian
P1.	21	3				American Indian and Alaska Native; Native Hawaiian and Other Pacific Islander
P1.	22	3				American Indian and Alaska Native; Some Other Race
P1.	23	3				Asian; Native Hawaiian and Other Pacific Islander
P1.	24	3				Asian; Some Other Race
P1.	25	3				Native Hawaiian and Other Pacific Islander; Some Other Race
P1.	26	2			Population of three races:	
P1.	27	3				White; Black or African American; American Indian and Alaska Native
P1.	28	3				White; Black or African American; Asian
P1.	29	3				White; Black or African American; Native Hawaiian and Other Pacific Islander
P1.	30	3				White; Black or African American; Some Other Race
P1.	31	3				White; American Indian and Alaska Native; Asian
P1.	32	3				White; American Indian and Alaska Native; Native Hawaiian and Other Pacific Islander
P1.	33	3				White; American Indian and Alaska Native; Some Other Race
P1.	34	3				White; Asian; Native Hawaiian and Other Pacific Islander
P1.	35	3				White; Asian; Some Other Race
P1.	36	3				White; Native Hawaiian and Other Pacific Islander; Some Other Race

Table No.	Cell Count	Indent				
P1.	37	3				Black or African American; American Indian and Alaska Native; Asian
P1.	38	3				Black or African American; American Indian and Alaska Native; Native Hawaiian and Other Pacific Islander
P1.	39	3				Black or African American; American Indian and Alaska Native; Some Other Race
P1.	40	3				Black or African American; Asian; Native Hawaiian and Other Pacific Islander
P1.	41	3				Black or African American; Asian; Some Other Race
P1.	42	3				Black or African American; Native Hawaiian and Other Pacific Islander; Some Other Race
P1.	43	3				American Indian and Alaska Native; Asian; Native Hawaiian and Other Pacific Islander
P1.	44	3				American Indian and Alaska Native; Asian; Some Other Race
P1.	45	3				American Indian and Alaska Native; Native Hawaiian and Other Pacific Islander; Some Other Race
P1.	46	3				Asian; Native Hawaiian and Other Pacific Islander; Some Other Race
P1.	47	2			Population of four races:	
P1.	48	3				White; Black or African American; American Indian and Alaska Native; Asian
P1.	49	3				White; Black or African American; American Indian and Alaska Native; Native Hawaiian and Other Pacific Islander
P1.	50	3				White; Black or African American; American Indian and Alaska Native; Some Other Race
P1.	51	3				White; Black or African American; Asian; Native Hawaiian and Other Pacific Islander
P1.	52	3				White; Black or African American; Asian; Some Other Race
P1.	53	3				White; Black or African American; Native Hawaiian and Other Pacific Islander; Some Other Race
P1.	54	3				White; American Indian and Alaska Native; Asian; Native Hawaiian and Other Pacific Islander
P1.	55	3				White; American Indian and Alaska Native; Asian; Some Other Race
P1.	56	3				White; American Indian and Alaska Native; Native Hawaiian and Other Pacific Islander; Some Other Race
P1.	57	3				White; Asian; Native Hawaiian and Other Pacific Islander; Some Other Race

(Continued).

Table No.	Cell Count	Indent	
P1.	58	3	Black or African American; American Indian and Alaska Native; Asian; Native Hawaiian and Other Pacific Islander
P1.	59	3	Black or African American; American Indian and Alaska Native; Asian; Some Other Race
P1.	60	3	Black or African American; American Indian and Alaska Native; Native Hawaiian and Other Pacific Islander; Some Other Race
P1.	61	3	Black or African American; Asian; Native Hawaiian and Other Pacific Islander; Some Other Race
P1.	62	3	American Indian and Alaska Native; Asian; Native Hawaiian and Other Pacific Islander; Some Other Race
P1.	63	2	Population of five races:
P1.	64	3	White; Black or African American; American Indian and Alaska Native; Asian; Native Hawaiian and Other Pacific Islander
P1.	65	3	White; Black or African American; American Indian and Alaska Native; Asian; Some Other Race
P1.	66	3	White; Black or African American; American Indian and Alaska Native; Native Hawaiian and Other Pacific Islander; Some Other Race
P1.	67	3	White; Black or African American; Asian; Native Hawaiian and Other Pacific Islander; Some Other Race
P1.	68	3	White; American Indian and Alaska Native; Asian; Native Hawaiian and Other Pacific Islander; Some Other Race
P1.	69	3	Black or African American; American Indian and Alaska Native; Asian; Native Hawaiian and Other Pacific Islander; Some Other Race
P1.	70	2	Population of six races:
P1.	71	3	White; Black or African American; American Indian and Alaska Native; Asian; Native Hawaiian and Other Pacific Islander; Some Other Race

Table No.	Cell Count	Indent	
P2.		0	HISPANIC OR LATINO, AND NOT HISPANIC OR LATINO BY RACE [73]
P2.		0	Universe: Total population
P2.	1	0	Total:
P2.	2	1	Hispanic or Latino
P2.	3	1	Not Hispanic or Latino:
P2.	4	2	Population of one race:
P2.	5	3	White alone
P2.	6	3	Black or African American alone
P2.	7	3	American Indian and Alaska Native alone
P2.	8	3	Asian alone
P2.	9	3	Native Hawaiian and Other Pacific Islander alone
P2.	10	3	Some Other Race alone
P2.	11	2	Two or More Races:
P2.	12	3	Population of two races:
P2.	13	4	White; Black or African American
P2.	14	4	White; American Indian and Alaska Native
P2.	15	4	White; Asian
P2.	16	4	White; Native Hawaiian and Other Pacific Islander
P2.	17	4	White; Some Other Race
P2.	18	4	Black or African American; American Indian and Alaska Native
P2.	19	4	Black or African American; Asian

(Continued).

Table No.	Cell Count	Indent	
P2.	20	4	Black or African American; Native Hawaiian and Other Pacific Islander
P2.	21	4	Black or African American; Some Other Race
P2.	22	4	American Indian and Alaska Native; Asian
P2.	23	4	American Indian and Alaska Native; Native Hawaiian and Other Pacific Islander
P2.	24	4	American Indian and Alaska Native; Some Other Race
P2.	25	4	Asian; Native Hawaiian and Other Pacific Islander
P2.	26	4	Asian; Some Other Race
P2.	27	4	Native Hawaiian and Other Pacific Islander; Some Other Race
<CONTINUED>			
P4.		0	HISPANIC OR LATINO, AND NOT HISPANIC OR LATINO BY RACE FOR THE POPULATION 18 YEARS AND OVER [73]
P4.		0	Universe: Total population 18 years and over
P4.	1	0	Total:
P4.	2	1	Hispanic or Latino
P4.	3	1	Not Hispanic or Latino:
P4.	4	2	Population of one race:
P4.	5	3	White alone
P4.	6	3	Black or African American alone
P4.	7	3	American Indian and Alaska Native alone

Table No.	Cell Count	Indent	Description
P4.	8	3	Asian alone
P4.	9	3	Native Hawaiian and Other Pacific Islander alone
P4.	10	3	Some Other Race alone
P4.	11	2	Two or More Races:
P4.	12	3	Population of two races:
P4.	13	4	White; Black or African American
P4.	14	4	White; American Indian and Alaska Native
P4.	15	4	White; Asian
P4.	16	4	White; Native Hawaiian and Other Pacific Islander
P4.	17	4	White; Some Other Race
P4.	18	4	Black or African American; American Indian and Alaska Native
P4.	19	4	Black or African American; Asian
P4.	20	4	Black or African American; Native Hawaiian and Other Pacific Islander
P4.	21	4	Black or African American; Some Other Race
P4.	22	4	American Indian and Alaska Native; Asian
P4.	23	4	American Indian and Alaska Native; Native Hawaiian and Other Pacific Islander
P4.	24	4	American Indian and Alaska Native; Some Other Race
P4.	25	4	Asian; Native Hawaiian and Other Pacific Islander
P4.	26	4	Asian; Some Other Race
P4.	27	4	Native Hawaiian and Other Pacific Islander; Some Other Race
P1.	66	3	White; Black or African American; American Indian and Alaska Native; Native Hawaiian and Other Pacific Islander; Some Other Race

(Continued).

Table No.	Cell Count	Indent	
P1.	67	3	White; Black or African American; Asian; Native Hawaiian and Other Pacific Islander; Some Other Race
P1.	68	3	White; American Indian and Alaska Native; Asian; Native Hawaiian and Other Pacific Islander; Some Other Race
P1.	69	3	Black or African American; American Indian and Alaska Native; Asian; Native Hawaiian and Other Pacific Islander; Some Other Race
P1.	70	2	Population of six races:
P1.	71	3	White; Black or African American; American Indian and Alaska Native; Asian; Native Hawaiian and Other Pacific Islander; Some Other Race
P2.		0	HISPANIC OR LATINO, AND NOT HISPANIC OR LATINO BY RACE [73]
P2.		0	Universe: Total population
P2.	1	0	Total:
P2.	2	1	Hispanic or Latino
P2.	3	1	Not Hispanic or Latino:
P2.	4	2	Population of one race:
P2.	5	3	White alone
P2.	6	3	Black or African American alone
P2.	7	3	American Indian and Alaska Native alone
P2.	8	3	Asian alone
P2.	9	3	Native Hawaiian and Other Pacific Islander alone

Table No.	Cell Count	Indent	
P2.	10	3	Some Other Race alone
P2.	11	2	Two or More Races:
P2.	12	3	Population of two races:
P2.	13	4	White; Black or African American
P2.	14	4	White; American Indian and Alaska Native
P2.	15	4	White; Asian
P2.	16	4	White; Native Hawaiian and Other Pacific Islander
P2.	17	4	White; Some Other Race
P2.	18	4	Black or African American; American Indian and Alaska Native
P2.	19	4	Black or African American; Asian
P2.	20	4	Black or African American; Native Hawaiian and Other Pacific Islander
P2.	21	4	Black or African American; Some Other Race
P2.	22	4	American Indian and Alaska Native; Asian
P2.	23	4	American Indian and Alaska Native; Native Hawaiian and Other Pacific Islander
P2.	24	4	American Indian and Alaska Native; Some Other Race
P2.	25	4	Asian; Native Hawaiian and Other Pacific Islander
P2.	26	4	Asian; Some Other Race
P2.	27	4	Native Hawaiian and Other Pacific Islander; Some Other Race
P4.		0	HISPANIC OR LATINO, AND NOT HISPANIC OR LATINO BY RACE FOR THE POPULATION 18 YEARS AND OVER [73]
P4.		0	Universe: Total population 18 years and over

(Continued).

Table No.	Cell Count	Indent	
P4.	1	0	Total:
P4.	2	1	Hispanic or Latino
P4.	3	1	Not Hispanic or Latino:
P4.	4	2	Population of one race:
P4.	5	3	White alone
P4.	6	3	Black or African American alone
P4.	7	3	American Indian and Alaska Native alone
P4.	8	3	Asian alone
P4.	9	3	Native Hawaiian and Other Pacific Islander alone
P4.	10	3	Some Other Race alone
P4.	11	2	Two or More Races:
P4.	12	3	Population of two races:
P4.	13	4	White; Black or African American
P4.	14	4	White; American Indian and Alaska Native
P4.	15	4	White; Asian
P4.	16	4	White; Native Hawaiian and Other Pacific Islander
P4.	17	4	White; Some Other Race
P4.	18	4	Black or African American; American Indian and Alaska Native
P4.	19	4	Black or African American; Asian
P4.	20	4	Black or African American; Native Hawaiian and Other Pacific Islander

Table No.	Cell Count	Indent	
P4.	21	4	Black or African American; Some Other Race
P4.	22	4	American Indian and Alaska Native; Asian
P4.	23	4	American Indian and Alaska Native; Native Hawaiian and Other Pacific Islander
P4.	24	4	American Indian and Alaska Native; Some Other Race
P4.	25	4	Asian; Native Hawaiian and Other Pacific Islander
P4.	26	4	Asian; Some Other Race
P4.	27	4	Native Hawaiian and Other Pacific Islander; Some Other Race
H1.		0	OCCUPANCY STATUS [3]
H1.		0	Universe: Housing units
H1.	1	0	Total:
H1.	2	1	Occupied
H1.	3	1	Vacant

2010 P.L. 94-171 Redistricting Data Products Delivery Timeline

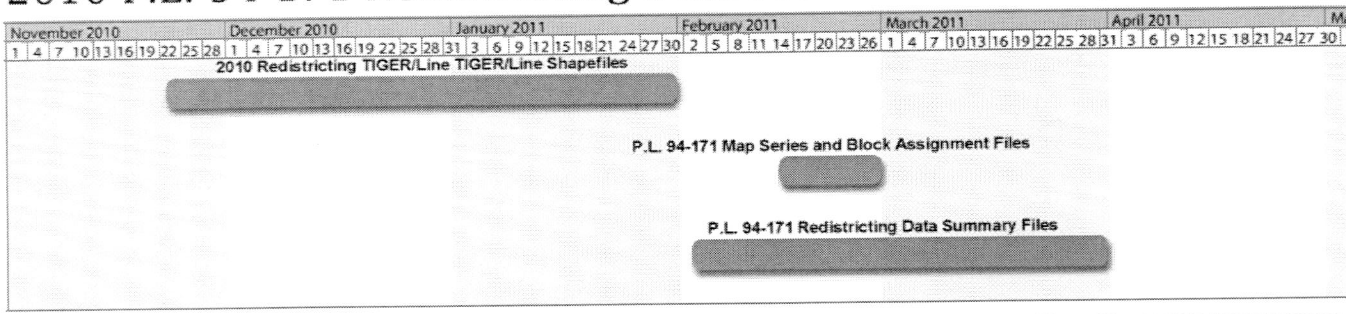

The 2010 Redistricting TIGER/Line® Shapefiles are spatial extracts from the Census Bureau's MAF/TIGER database. These files contain linear features such as roads, railroads, rivers as well as geographies such as American Indian reservations, places, census tracts, census block groups, and census blocks, in addition to many others.

The 2010 P.L. 94-171 Map Series includes County Block Maps, Census Tract Reference Maps, School District Reference Maps, and Voting District Reference Maps.

The 2010 P.L. 94-171 Redistricting Data Summary Files will include four population tables, including total population, total population by race, ethnicity, and voting age (18+). In addition, for the 2010 Census, this file will include a table on occupancy status of housing units

Where to Go to Learn More!

Responsive government at all levels begins with legislative boundaries that reflect an accurate count of the population. We hope this brochure helps you better understand the data and maps that the Census Bureau provides and how you can use them in redistricting. You can learn more about the design and content of other Census Bureau data products from the Census Bureau's Web site, particularly the American FactFinder. Just point your browser to <www.census.gov>. More information about the 2010 Census Redistricting Data Program, can be obtained by calling 301-763-4039 or sending e-mail to <catherine.clark.mccully@census.gov> or <james.whitehorne@census.gov>. You also may write to:

U.S. Census Bureau,
Redistricting Data Offce, HQ – 8H019
Washington, DC 20233.

For more information on redistricting data, access the the Redistricting Data Offce Web page located at <www.census.gov/rdo> and click on "Redistricting Data" or access the National Conference of State Legislatures Web site at <www.ncsl.org>.

Cathy McCully
Chief
Census Redistricting Data Offce
catherine.clark.mccully@census.gov
301-763-4039

James Whitehorne
Assistant Chief
Census Redistricting Data Offce
james.whitehorne@census.gov
301-763-4039

The House of Representatives... ISBN: 978-1-61324-308-4
Editors: R. D. Orsino, O. G. Trance

Chapter 13

CONGRESSIONAL REDISTRICTING: THE CONSTITUTIONALITY OF CREATING AN AT-LARGE DISTRICT*

L. Paige Whitaker

SUMMARY

This report discusses the constitutionality of legislation, such as the District of Columbia House Voting Rights Act of 2009, H.R. 157 (111th Congress), that would create an at-large congressional district. While it is not without doubt, based on the authority granted to Congress under the Constitution to regulate congressional elections and relevant Supreme Court precedent, it appears that federal law establishing a temporary at-large congressional district would likely be upheld as constitutional.

H.R. 157, among other provisions, would expand the U.S. House of Representatives by two members to a total of 437 members. The first of these two new seats would be allocated to create a voting member representing the District of Columbia. The second seat would be assigned in accordance with 2000 census data and existing federal law, resulting in the addition of a fourth congressional seat in the state of Utah that would be a temporary at-large district.

On March 2, 2009, the House Judiciary Committee reported the bill, as amended (H.Rept. 111- 22), but no further action was taken by the

* This is an edited, reformatted and augmented version of a Congressional Research Services publication, dated December 28, 2010.

House. On February 26, 2009, the Senate passed a related bill, S. 160, by a vote of 61-37. During the 110th Congress, the House passed similar legislation, H.R. 1905, by a vote of 241 to 177. A companion bill, S. 1257, was considered by the Senate, but a motion to invoke cloture failed by a vote of 57 to 42.

H.R. 157 (111TH CONGRESS), THE DISTRICT OF COLUMBIA HOUSE VOTING RIGHTS ACT OF 2009

On March 2, 2009, the House Judiciary Committee reported the District of Columbia House Voting Rights Act of 2009, H.R. 157 (111th Congress). The bill, as amended (H.Rept. 111-22), among other provisions, would expand the U.S. House of Representatives by two members to a total of 437 members.[1] The first of these two new seats would be allocated to create a voting member representing the District of Columbia. The second seat would be assigned in accordance with 2000 census data and existing federal law,[2] resulting in the addition of a fourth congressional seat in the state of Utah that would be a temporary at-large district.

No further action was taken by the House. On February 26, 2009, the Senate passed a related bill, S. 160, by a vote of 61-37. During the 110th Congress, the House passed similar legislation, H.R. 1905, by a vote of 241 to 177. A similar bill, S. 1257, was considered by the Senate, but a motion to invoke cloture failed by a vote of 57 to 42.

This report discusses the constitutionality of the aspect of this legislation that would create an at-large congressional district.

BRIEF CONSTITUTIONAL ANALYSIS

The U.S. Constitution provides the states with primary authority over congressional elections, but grants Congress the final authority over most aspects of such elections. This congressional power is at its most broad in the case of House elections, which have historically been decided by a system of popular voting.[3] Article I, § 4, cl. 1 provides that

> The Times, Places and Manner of holding Elections for Senators and Representatives, shall be prescribed in each State by the Legislature

> thereof; but the Congress may at any time by Law make or alter such Regulations, except as to the Places of chusing Senators.[4]

The Supreme Court and lower courts have interpreted this language to mean that Congress has extensive power to regulate most elements of congressional elections,[5] including a broad authority to protect the integrity of those elections.[6]

The Constitution does not specify how members of the House are to be elected once they are apportioned to a state. Originally, most states having more than one Representative divided their territory into geographic districts, permitting only one member of Congress to be elected from each district. Other states, however, allowed House candidates to run at-large or from multi-member districts or from some combination of the two. In those states employing single-member districts, however, the problem of gerrymandering, the practice of drawing district lines in order to maximize political party advantage, quickly arose.[7]

Accordingly, Congress began establishing standards for House districts. Congress first passed federal redistricting standards in 1842, when it added a requirement to the apportionment act of that year that Representatives "should be elected by districts composed of contiguous territory equal in number to the number of Representatives to which each said state shall be entitled, no one district electing more than one Representative." (5 Stat. 491.)[8] The Apportionment Act of 1872 added another requirement to those first set out in 1842, stating that districts should contain "as nearly as practicable an equal number of inhabitants." (17 Stat. 492.) A further requirement of "compact territory" was added when the Apportionment Act of 1901 was adopted stating that districts must be made up of "contiguous and compact territory and containing as nearly as practicable an equal number of inhabitants." (26 Stat. 736.)[9] Although these standards were never enforced if the states failed to meet them, this language was repeated in the 1911 Apportionment Act and remained in effect until 1929, with the adoption of the Permanent Apportionment Act, which did not include any districting standards. After 1929, there were no congressionally imposed standards governing congressional redistricting; in 1941, however, Congress enacted a law providing for various contingencies if states failed to redistrict after a census—including at-large representation. (55 Stat 761.) In 1967, Congress reimposed the requirement that Representatives must run from single-member districts, rather than running at-large. (81 Stat. 581.)

Both the 1941 and 1967 laws are still in effect, codified at 2 U.S.C. §§ 2a and 2c. In *Branch v. Smith*,[10] the Supreme Court considered the operation and inherent tension between these two provisions.[11] The question of congressional authority was not in dispute in this litigation. Rather, the Court noted in passing that the current statutory scheme governing apportionment of the House of Representatives was enacted in 1929 pursuant to congressional authority under the "Times, Places and Manner" provision of the Constitution. Consequently, it seems likely that Congress has broad authority, within specified constitutional parameters, to establish how members' districts will be established, including the creation of at-large districts.

It might be suggested that creating an at-large congressional district in a state could violate the "one person, one vote" standard established by the Supreme Court in *Wesberry v. Sanders.*[12] In *Wesberry*, the Supreme Court first applied the one person, one vote standard in the context of evaluating the constitutionality of a Georgia congressional redistricting statute that created a district with two to three times as many residents as the state's other nine districts. In striking down the statute, the Court held that Article I, section 2, clause 1, providing that Representatives be chosen "by the People of the several States" and be "apportioned among the several States ... according to their respective Numbers," requires that "as nearly as is practicable, one man's vote in a congressional election is to be worth as much as another's."[13]

While it is not beyond dispute, it does not appear that the creation of an at-large district under the circumstances outlined in H.R. 157 would be interpreted to create a conflict with the "one person, one vote" standard. Under H.R. 157, each Utah voter would have the opportunity to vote both for a candidate to represent his or her congressional district *as well as* for a candidate to represent the state at-large. Each person's vote for an at-large candidate would be of equal worth. Further, each person's vote for an at-large candidate would not affect the value of his or her vote for a candidate representing a congressional district. Accordingly, all Utah residents' votes would have equal value, thereby arguably comporting with the one person, one vote principle.

Based on the authority granted to Congress under the Constitution to regulate congressional elections and relevant Supreme Court precedent, it appears that a federal law establishing a temporary at-large congressional district would likely be upheld as constitutional.

End Notes

1 H.R. 157 (111th Cong.) § 3(a).

2 *Id.* at § 2.

3 U.S. CONST. Art. I, §2, cl. 1 provides that "[t]he House of Representatives shall be composed of Members chosen every second Year by the People of the several States."

4 U.S. CONST. Art. I, §4, cl. 1.

5 285 U.S. at 366. *See* United States v. Gradwell, 243 U.S. 476, 483 (1917) (finding that Congress has full authority over the federal election process, from registration to certification of results); United States v. Mosley, 238 U.S. 383, 386 (1915) (holding that Congress has the authority to enforce the right to cast a ballot and have a ballot counted); In re Coy, 127 U.S. 731, 752 (1888)(determining that Congress has authority to regulate conduct at any election coinciding with a federal contest); Ex parte Yarbrough, 110 U.S. 651, 662 (1884) (holding that Congress has the authority to make additional laws for free, pure, and safe exercise of the right to vote).

6 For example, the Supreme Court has noted that the right to vote for members of Congress is derived from the Constitution and that Congress may therefore legislate broadly under this provision to protect the integrity of this right. *See* Smiley v. Holm, 285 U.S. 355, 366 (1932). Furthermore, the Court in *Smiley* found that the authority to regulate the "times, places and manner" of federal elections: embrace[s] [the] authority to provide a complete code for congressional elections, not only as to times and places, but in relation to notices, registration, supervision of voting, protection of voters, prevention of fraud and corrupt practices, counting of votes, duties of inspectors and canvassers, and making and publication of election returns; in short, to enact the numerous requirements as to procedure and safeguards which experience shows are necessary in order to enforce the fundamental right involved.... [Congress] has a general supervisory power over the whole subject. *Id.*

7 The term "gerrymander" originated in 1812 when an odd shaped congressional district, which resembled a salamander, was created by the Massachusetts legislature. In a play on words it was referred to as a gerrymander, named after Elbridge Gerry, then governor of Massachusetts. CONGRESSIONAL QUARTERLY INC., CONGRESSIONAL DISTRICTS IN THE 1980S 617 (M.V. Gottron, ed. 1983).

8 In 1843, three states elected their delegations at-large. At the beginning of the 28th Congress, the Clerk of the House declined to entertain a motion to exclude them and the at-large Representatives were sworn in. After the delegations were seated, the House directed the Committee of Elections "to examine and report upon the certificates of elections, or the credentials of the Members returned to serve in this House." The Committee report found the 1842 law to be "not a law made in pursuance of the Constitution of the United States, and valid, operative, and [therefore not] binding on the states." Later the House adopted a resolution declaring the Representatives of the states "duly elected," but omitted any mention of the apportionment law. *See* Asher C. Hinds, *Hinds' Precedents of the House of Representatives of the United States* (Washington: GPO, 1907), at 170-173. In 1861, California elected three Representatives at-large, and they too were seated. *See Hinds, supra,* at 182. More recently, for example, during the 89th Congress in 1965, Maryland elected one Representative at-large (in addition to seven Representatives from districts); Texas elected one Representative at-large (in addition to 23 Representatives from districts); and Hawaii elected both of its two Representatives at-large, all of whom were seated. *See Biographical Directory of the United States Congress* 1774-2005, H.R. DOC. NO. 108-222 at 431-35.

[9] 46 Stat. 21.

[10] 538 U.S. 254 (2003).

[11] The 1967 law, codified at 2 U.S.C. § 2c, requiring single-member districts, appears to conflict with the 1941 law, codified a 2 U.S.C § 2a(c), which provides options for at-large representation if a state fails to create new districts after the reapportionment of seats following a census. The apparent contradictions may be explained by the somewhat confusing legislative history of P.L. 90-196 (1967) (2 U.S.C. § 2c), prohibiting at-large elections. In 1941 and 1967, Congress enacted modifications to the apportionment statute at 2 U.S.C. §§ 2a(c) and 2c, respectively. The *Branch* Court reconciled the inherent tension between the two provisions by holding that the provision requiring at-large elections under § 2a(c) was subject to the requirement under § 2c that single-member districts must be drawn whenever possible. *Id.* at 266-71. For further discussion, *see* CRS Report RS21585, *Congressional Redistricting: Is At-Large Representation Permitted in the House of Representatives?*, by David C. Huckabee and L. Paige Whitaker.

[12] 376 U.S. 1 (1964).

[13] *Id.* at 7-8. Therefore, the Court held that, due to such substantial population deviations among the congressional districts, the statute "grossly" discriminated against certain voters by contracting the value of some votes and expanding that of others. *Id.* at 7. While it may be impossible to draw congressional district lines with precise mathematical equality, the Court determined that a maximum variance of 30.26% is unconstitutional. Under Article I, section 2, the Court announced, congressional districts must be "equal in population as nearly as practicable." *Id.* at 18.

The House of Representatives... ISBN: 978-1-61324-308-4
Editors: R. D. Orsino, O. G. Trance

Chapter 14

CONGRESSIONAL REDISTRICTING: A LEGAL ANALYSIS OF THE SUPREME COURT RULING IN *LEAGUE OF UNITED LATIN AMERICAN CITIZENS (LULAC) V. PERRY*[*]

L. Paige Whitaker

SUMMARY

In a splintered, complex decision, the U.S. Supreme Court in *League of United Latin American Citizens (LULAC) v. Perry* largely upheld a Texas congressional redistricting plan that was drawn mid-decade against claims of unconstitutional partisan gerrymandering. The Court invalidated one Texas congressional district, District 23, finding that it diluted the voting power of Latinos in violation of Section 2 of the Voting Rights Act. While not ruling out the possibility of a claim of partisan gerrymandering being within the scope of judicial review, a majority of the Court in this case was unable to find a "reliable" standard for making such a determination.

In the 111th Congress, H.R. 3025, the "Fairness and Independence in Redistricting Act of 2009," (Representative Tanner) and S. 1332, the "Fairness and Independence in Redistricting Act of 2009," (Senator Johnson) are

---

[*] This is an edited, reformatted and augmented version of a Congressional Research Services publication, dated January 12, 2010.

pending. These bills would, among other things, prohibit states from carrying out more than one congressional redistricting after a decennial census and apportionment, unless a court required the state to conduct subsequent redistricting to comply with the Constitution or to enforce the Voting Rights Act; require states to conduct redistricting through the use of independent commissions; and impose standards of compactness, contiguity, and geographical continuity.

BACKGROUND

Following the 2000 census, Texas was apportioned two additional congressional seats. Subsequently, the state legislature was unable to enact a redistricting map, resulting in litigation and, ultimately, imposition of a court-ordered congressional redistricting plan.[1] The 2002 election was held under the court-ordered plan, resulting in a Democratic majority in the Texas congressional delegation. In October 2003, after the Republican party gained control of the Texas State House of Representatives, and thus, both houses of the legislature, it enacted a new congressional redistricting map with the goal "to increase [Republican] representation in the congressional delegation."[2] The League of United Latin American Citizens (LULAC) and others challenged the new plan in court, alleging various statutory and constitutional violations. The district court entered judgment against LULAC on all claims,[3] and they appealed to the U.S. Supreme Court. As the Court had just issued its decision in *Vieth v. Jubelirer*,[4] it vacated the district court decision and remanded in light of its holding in *Vieth*. On remand, the district court again ruled against LULAC, finding that the scope of its consideration was limited to questions of political gerrymandering.[5] In their appeal to the Supreme Court, appellants argued that the new redistricting plan should be invalidated as an unconstitutional partisan gerrymander.

ANALYSIS OF SUPREME COURT RULING

League of United Latin American Citizens (LULAC) v. Perry was a consolidation of four appeals before the U.S. Supreme Court.[6] In this ruling, the Supreme Court's nine Justices filed six different opinions, each with subparts. Many issues were raised by the appellants in this case, but the decision primarily addressed two topics: (1) the constitutionality of partisan gerrymandering and (2) whether the Texas redistricting plan violated Section 2 of the Voting Rights Act.

Constitutionality of Partisan Gerrymandering

While not ruling out the possibility of a claim of unconstitutional partisan gerrymandering being within the scope of judicial review, the Court in *LULAC v. Perry* was unable to find a sufficient standard for making such a determination.

Appellants in *LULAC* challenged the 2003 mid-decennial Texas redistricting plan on the grounds that it was an unconstitutional political gerrymander motivated by partisan objectives, in violation of equal protection and First Amendment guarantees under the Constitution. They maintained that the plan served no legitimate public purpose and burdened one group because of its political opinions and affiliation. Appellants urged the Court to adopt a rule or presumption of invalidity when a mid-decade redistricting plan is enacted solely for partisan purposes, thereby alleviating the need for courts to inquire about (or for parties to prove) the discriminatory effects of partisan gerrymandering.[7]

In evaluating appellants' arguments, the Court first noted that there were indications that "partisan motives did not dictate the plan in its entirety."[8] The Court further determined that ascertaining the legality of an act arising from "mixed motives" can be complicated, and indeed, "hazardous," particularly when the actor is a legislature and the act is a series of choices. Hence, the Court expressed skepticism of a claim seeking to invalidate a statute based on a legislature's unlawful motive without reference to its content. Notwithstanding its skepticism, the Court also found that in order for a claim of unconstitutional partisan gerrymandering to prevail, it must show a burden on complainants' representational rights, "as measured by a reliable standard." Indeed, the Court noted, for this exact reason, a majority of the *Vieth* Court had rejected a test "markedly similar" to the one proposed by the appellants.[9]

In regard to appellants' reliance on the fact that the redistricting plan was enacted mid-decade, the Court announced that the Constitution and the Court's case law "indicate that there is nothing inherently suspect about a legislature's decision to replace, mid-decade, a court-ordered plan with one of its own." Even if there were, the Court commented, "the fact of mid-decade redistricting alone is no sure indication of unlawful political gerrymanders."[10] The Court also observed that the "sole-intent standard" is no more compelling when bolstered by the fact that the redistricting was enacted mid-decade.[11]

Appellants proffered a second political gerrymandering theory: that mid-decade redistricting for exclusively partisan purposes violates the Constitution's one-person, one-vote requirement. Citing landmark Supreme Court holdings in *Karcher v. Daggett*[12] and *Kirkpatrick v. Preisler*,[13] they observed that population variances among congressional districts are acceptable only if they are "unavoidable," despite good faith efforts to attain complete equality "or for which justification is shown." From that premise, appellants maintained that due to population shifts in Texas since the 2000 census, the 2003 redistricting, which still relied on the 2000 census numbers, created unlawful population variances among the districts. To distinguish the Texas 2003 redistricting plan's reliance on three-year-old census numbers from other, more typical redistricting plans' reliance on three-year-old (or older) census numbers, appellants again highlighted the "voluntary, mid-decade" nature of the redistricting and its "partisan motivation." The Court found that the appellants' theory merely restated their primary argument that it was impermissible for the Texas legislature to redraw the districting map, mid-decade, for solely partisan purposes. Hence, for the same reasons it had originally rejected this argument, the Court once again found it unpersuasive. In its concluding statement, the Court announced:

> In sum, we disagree with appellants' view that a legislature's decision to override a valid, court-drawn plan mid-decade is sufficiently suspect to give shape to a reliable standard for identifying unconstitutional political gerrymanders. We conclude that appellants have established no legally impermissible use of political classifications. For this reason, they state no claim on which relief may be granted for their statewide challenge.[14]

Writing for the Court, Justice Kennedy announced that a majority of the Justices were unable to find a "reliable measure" of what constitutes unconstitutional partisan gerrymandering and therefore determined that the claims presented were not justiciable.[15] Notably, however, a majority of the Court stopped short of concluding that standards a court could use to evaluate such claims do not exist, which left existing Court precedent basically unchanged.

In the 2004 Supreme Court case of *Vieth v. Jubelirer,*[16] a plurality of four justices argued that claims of unconstitutional partisan gerrymandering are not justiciable[17] while another plurality of four justices maintained that such claims are justiciable, but were unable to agree upon a standard that courts could use in order to make such determinations.[18] The deciding vote in *Vieth*, Justice Kennedy, determined that the claims presented were not justiciable, but left open the possibility that such standards might exist.[19]

Similar to its decision in *Vieth,* the Court in *LULAC* was also divided into three camps on the issue of whether partisan gerrymandering claims are beyond the scope of judicial review. In *LULAC*, the same four justices from *Vieth* argued that claims of unconstitutional partisan gerrymandering are justiciable, while not agreeing upon a standard for adjudicating such claims.[20] Of the four justices in *Vieth* who believed that such claims are not justiciable, the two who remain on the Court maintained that same position in *LULAC*.[21] Two justices who joined the Court since its ruling in *Vieth,* Chief Justice Roberts and Justice Alito, generally agreed with Justice Kennedy's position, leaving open the possibility that the Court might discern a standard for adjudicating unconstitutional partisan gerrymandering claims in a future case.[22]

As a result, a majority of the Court in *LULAC* was unable to find a "reliable measure" of what constitutes an unconstitutional partisan gerrymandering. Therefore, the Court determined that the claims presented in this case were not justiciable,[23] but declined to conclude that standards a court could use to evaluate such claims do not exist. In the aftermath of *LULAC*, it appears theoretically possible for a claim of unconstitutional partisan gerrymandering to prevail. However, the critical standard that a court could use to ascertain such a determination and grant relief remains unresolved.

Compliance with the Voting Rights Act

Appellants in *LULAC* argued that changes to Texas's congressional District 23 diluted the voting rights of Latinos who remained in the district after the 2003 redistricting, causing the Latino share of the citizen voting-age population to drop from 57.5% to 46%, in violation of Section 2 of the Voting Rights Act. Although the Supreme Court acknowledged the district court's finding that Latino voting strength was unquestionably weakened, the question for the Court was whether it constituted vote dilution.

Engaging in a threshold analysis for establishing a Section 2 violation in accordance with its landmark decision, *Thornburg v. Gingles,*[24] the Court determined that appellants satisfied all three *Gingles* requirements; that is, District 23 possessed the requisite cohesion among the Latino minority group, bloc voting among the majority population, and a Latino citizenry that was "sufficiently large and geographically compact to constitute a majority in a single-member district."[25] Nevertheless, the appellee argued that it met its Section 2 obligations by creating a new District 25 as an "offsetting opportunity" district. Noting that it has rejected the premise that a state can compensate for the "less-than-equal" opportunity of some individuals by providing greater opportunity to others, the Court rejected the appellee's argument.[26]

Next, as directed by the text of Section 2 of the Voting Rights Act,[27] the Court turned to consider the "totality of the circumstances" to determine whether members of the Latino population have less opportunity than other members of the electorate to participate in the political process and to elect candidates of their choice. The Court determined that changes to District 23 stymied the progress of a racial group that had historically been subject to substantial voting-related discrimination and was increasingly politically active and cohesive. In effect, the Court noted, "the State took away the Latinos' opportunity because Latinos were about to exercise it."[28] The Court further announced that the state "chose to break apart a Latino opportunity district to protect the incumbent congressman from the growing dissatisfaction of the cohesive and politically active Latino community in the district." Then, purporting to compensate for the injury, the state created an entirely new district, combining two groups of Latinos, geographically far apart and representing differing communities of interest. Even assuming that the redrawing of District 23 was close to proportional representation, the Court held that "its troubling blend of politics and race—and the resulting vote dilution of a group that was beginning to achieve §2's goal of overcoming prior electoral discrimination—cannot be sustained."[29]

Accordingly, the Supreme Court ruled that District 23 violated Section 2 of the Voting Rights Act because it diluted the voting power of Latinos. This portion of the opinion was written by Justice Kennedy and joined by Justices Souter, Ginsburg, Stevens, and Breyer.

CONSEQUENCES

After rejecting the statewide challenge to Texas's redistricting as an unconstitutional partisan gerrymander, and holding that congressional District 23 violates Section 2 of the Voting Rights Act, the Supreme Court in *LULAC* remanded the case for further proceedings.[30] In accordance with the Supreme

Court's ruling, on June 29, 2006, a federal district court in Texas ordered parties in the case to submit remedial proposals, including supporting maps and briefs.[31] The court heard oral argument on August 3 and adopted a new plan on August 4 redrawing Texas congressional districts 15, 21, 23, 25, and 28. The court ordered that special elections in the redrawn districts for the 110th Congress be held in conjunction with the November 7, 2006, general election.[32]

As a result of the Court's ruling, commentators have observed other states may dispense with the tradition of redrawing congressional districts only once per decade following the decennial census, and instead, redistrict following a change in political control of the state government. It has also been noted, however, that there does not appear to be any urgency on the part of state legislatures to do so.[33]

SELECTED LEGISLATION IN THE 111TH CONGRESS

In the 111th Congress, H.R. 3025, the "Fairness and Independence in Redistricting Act of 2009," (Representative Tanner) and S. 1332, the "Fairness and Independence in Redistricting Act of 2009," (Senator Johnson) are pending. These bills would, among other things, prohibit states from carrying out more than one congressional redistricting after a decennial census and apportionment, unless a court required the state to conduct subsequent redistricting to comply with the Constitution or to enforce the Voting Rights Act; require states to conduct redistricting through the use of independent commissions; and impose standards of compactness, contiguity, and geographical continuity.

End Notes

1 *See* Balderas v. Texas, Civ. Action No. 6:01CV158 (ED Tex., Nov. 14, 2001) (per curiam), *summarily aff'd,* 536 U.S. 919 (2002).

2 *See* League of United Latin American Citizens (LULAC) v. Perry, 548 U.S. 399, 412 (2006) (plurality opinion) (quoting Session v. Perry, 298 F. Supp. 2d 451, 471 (2004) (per curiam)).

3 Session v. Perry, 298 F. Supp. 2d 451 (2004) (per curiam). NST-ann-est.html.

4 541 U.S. 267 (2004). The *Vieth* Court ruled that a constitutional equal protection challenge to a political gerrymander may be justiciable (i.e., within the scope of judicial review), but a majority of the Court was unable to agree on a standard to apply in making such a

determination. *See id.* at 127-37 (plurality opinion) and 161-62 (Powell, J., concurring in part, dissenting in part).

[5] Henderson v. Perry, 399 F. Supp. 2d 756 (2005).

[6] LULAC v. Perry, No. 05-204; Travis County, Texas v. Perry, No. 05-254; Jackson v. Perry, No. 05-276; and GI Forum of Texas v. Perry, No. 05-439.

[7] LULAC, 548 U.S. at 416-17 (2006).

[8] *Id.* at 417. The Court further noted, "The legislature does seem to have decided to redistrict with the sole purpose of achieving a Republican congressional majority, but partisan aims did not guide every line it drew." *Id.*

[9] *Id.* at 418 (citing Vieth v. Jubelirer, 541 U.S. 267 (2003)).

[10] *Id.* at 419.

[11] *Id.* at 418.

[12] 462 U.S. 725, 730 (1983).

[13] 394 U.S. 526, 531 (1969).

[14] LULAC, 548 U.S. at 423.

[15] *See id.* at 420.

[16] 541 U.S. 267 (2004) (plurality opinion).

[17] *See id.* at 271-306 (Scalia, J., joined by Chief Justice Rehnquist, and Justices O'Connor and Thomas) (arguing that Davis v. Bandemer, 478 U.S. 109 (1986), which held that claims of partisan political gerrymandering are justiciable, was wrongly decided because "no judicially discernible and manageable standards for adjudicating political gerrymandering claims have emerged"). *Id.* at 281.

[18] *See id.* at 317-41 (2004) (Stevens, J., dissenting); *id.* at 343-55 (Souter, J., dissenting, joined by Justice Ginsburg); *id.* at 355-68 (Breyer, J., dissenting).

[19] *See id.* at 306-17 (Kennedy, J., concurring).

[20] *See* LULAC, 548 U.S. at 447-83 (2006) (Stevens, J., dissenting in part, concurring in part); *id.* at 483-91 (Souter, J, concurring in part and dissenting in part, joined by Justice Ginsburg); *id.* at 491-92 (Breyer, J., concurring in part and dissenting in part).

[21] *See id.* at 511-20 (Scalia, J., dissenting, joined by Justice Thomas).

[22] *See id.* at 492-511 (Roberts, C.J., concurring in part, concurring in the judgment in part, dissenting in part, joined by Justice Alito).

[23] *See id.* at 446-47.

[24] 478 U.S. 30, 50 (1986)).

[25] LULAC, 548 U.S. at 425-28.

[26] *Id.* at 429 (citing Shaw v. Hunt (Shaw II), 517 U.S. 899, 917 (1996) (holding that vote dilution injuries are not remedied by creating a safe majority-black district elsewhere in the state)).

[27] *See* 42 U.S.C. § 1973(b).

[28] LULAC, 548 U.S. at 440.

[29] *Id.* at 442.

[30] *See id.* at 447.

[31] LULAC v. Perry, Civ. Action No. 2:03-CV-354 (ED Tex., June 29, 2006).

[32] LULAC v. Perry, Civ. Action No. 2:03-CV-354 (ED Tex., August 4, 2006).

[33] *See, e.g.,* Linda Greenhouse, *Justices Uphold Most Remapping in Texas by G.O.P.,* N.Y. TIMES, June 29, 2006.

INDEX

D

E

J

L

M

N

O

P

T

U

V

W

Y